Incline your ear and come unto me; hear that your soul may live
Is 55:3

W9-BZK-325

Engaging God's Word

1 & 2 Thessalonians

Engage Bible Studies

Tools That Transform

Engage Bible Studies

an imprint of

 COMMUNITY BIBLE STUDY

Engaging God's Word: 1 & 2 Thessalonians
Copyright © 2013 by Community Bible Study. All rights reserved.
ISBN 978-1-62194-018-0

Published by Community Bible Study
790 Stout Road
Colorado Springs, CO
1-800-826-4181
www.communitybiblestudy.org

Printed in the United States of America.

Contents

Introduction

Welcome to the life-changing adventure of engaging with God's Word! Whether this is the first time you've opened a Bible or you've studied the Scriptures all your life, good things are in store for you. Studying the Bible is unlike any other kind of study you have ever done. That's because the Word of God is *"living and active"* (Hebrews 4:12) and transcends time and cultures. The earth and heavens as we know them will one day pass away, but God's Word never will (Mark 13:31). It's as relevant to your life today as it was to the people who wrote it down centuries ago. And the fact that God's Word is living and active means that reading God's Word is always meant to be a personal experience. God's Word is not just dead words on a page—it is page after page of living, powerful words—so get ready, because the time you spend studying the Bible in this *Engaging God's Word* course will be life-transforming!

Why Study the Bible?

Some Christians read the Bible because they know they're supposed to. It's a good thing to do, and God expects it. And all that's true! However, there are many additional reasons to study God's Word. Here are just some of them.

We get to know God through His Word. Our God is a relational God who knows us and wants us to know Him. The Scriptures, which He authored, reveal much about Him: how He thinks and feels, what His purposes are, what He thinks about us, how He views the world He made, what He has planned for the future. The Bible shows us God's many attributes—His kindness, goodness, justice, love, faithfulness, mercy, compassion, creativity, redemption, sovereignty, and so on. As we get to know Him through His Word, we come to love and trust Him.

God speaks to us through His Word. One of the primary ways God speaks to us is through His written Word. Don't be surprised if, as you read the Bible, certain parts nearly jump off the page at you, almost as if they'd been written with you in mind. God is the Author of this incredible book, so that's not just possible, it's likely! Whether it is to find comfort, warning, correction, teaching, or guidance, always approach God's Word with your spiritual ears open (Isaiah 55:3) because God, your loving heavenly Father, has things He wants to say to you.

God's Word brings life. Just about everyone wants to learn the secret to "the good life." And the good news is, that secret is found in God's Word. Don't think of the Bible as a bunch of rules. Viewing it with that mindset is a distortion. God gave us His Word because as our Creator and the Creator of the universe, He alone knows how life was meant to work. He knows that love makes us happier than hate, that generosity brings more joy than greed, and that integrity allows us to rest more peacefully at night than deception does. God's ways are not always "easiest" but they are the way to life. As the Psalmist says, *"If Your law had not been my delight, I would have perished in my affliction. I will never forget Your precepts, for by them You have given me life"* (Psalm 119:92-93).

God's Word offers stability in an unstable world. Truth is an ever-changing negotiable for many people in our culture today. But building your life on constantly changing "truth" is like building your house on shifting sand. God's Word, like God Himself, never changes. What He says was true yesterday, is true today, and will still be true a billion years from now. Jesus said, *"Everyone then who hears these words of Mine and does them will be like a wise man who built his house on the rock"* (Matthew 7:24).

God's Word helps us to pray effectively. When we read God's Word and get to know what He is really like, we understand better how to pray. God answers prayers that are according to His will. We discover His will by reading the Bible. First John 5:14-15 tells us that *"this is the confidence that we have toward Him, that if we ask anything according to His will He hears us. And if we know that He hears us in whatever we ask, we know that we have the requests that we have asked of Him."*

How to Get the Most
out of *Engaging God's Word*

Each *Engaging God's Word* study contains key elements that have
been carefully designed to help you get the most out of your time in
God's Word. Slightly modified for your study-at-home success, this
approach is very similar to the tried-and-proven Bible study method that
Community Bible Study has used with thousands of men, women, and
children across the United States and around the world for nearly 40
years. There are some basic things you can expect to find in each course
in this series.

 ❖ Lesson 1 provides an overview of the Bible book (or books) you
    will study and questions to help you focus, anticipate, and pray
    about what you will be learning.

 ❖ Every lesson contains questions to answer on your own,
    commentary that reviews and clarifies the passage, and three
    special sections called "Apply what you have learned," "Think
    about" and "Personalize this lesson."

 ❖ Some lessons contain memory verse suggestions.

Whether you plan to use *Engaging God's Word* on your own or with a
group, here are some suggestions that will help you enjoy and receive the
most benefit from your study.

Spread out each lesson over several days. Your *Engaging God's Word*
lessons were designed to take a week to complete. Spreading out your
study rather than doing it all at once allows time for the things God is
teaching you to sink in and for you to practice applying them.

Pray each time you read God's Word. The Bible is a book unlike any
other because God Himself inspired it. The same Spirit who inspired
the human authors who wrote it will help you to understand and apply
it if you ask Him to. So make it a practice to ask Him to make His Word
come alive to you every time you read it.

Read the whole passage covered in the lesson. Before plunging into the questions, take time to read the specific chapter or verses that will be covered in that lesson. Doing this will give you important context for the whole lesson. Reading the Bible in context is an important principle in interpreting it accurately.

Begin learning the memory verse. Learning Scripture by heart requires discipline, but the rewards far outweigh the effort. Memorizing a verse allows you to recall it whenever you need it—for personal encouragement and direction, or to share with someone else. Consider writing the verse on a sticky note or index card that you can post where you will see it often or carry with you to review during the day. Reading and re-reading the verse often—out loud when possible—is a simple way to commit it to memory.

Re-read the passage for each section of questions. Each lesson is divided into sections so that you study one small part of Scripture at a time. Before attempting to answer the questions, review the verses that the questions will cover.

Answer the questions without consulting the Commentary or other reference materials. There is great joy in having the Holy Spirit teach you God's Word on your own, without the help of outside resources. Don't cheat yourself of the delight of discovery by reading the Commentary prematurely. Wait until after you've completed the lesson.

Repeat the process for all the question sections.

Prayerfully consider the "Apply what you have learned," marked with the ✇ push pin symbol. The vision of Community Bible Study is not to just gain knowledge about the Bible, but to be transformed by it. For this reason, each set of questions closes with a section that encourages you to apply what you are learning. Usually this section involves action—something for you to do. As you practice these suggestions, your life will change.

Read the Commentary. *Engaging God's Word* commentaries are written by theologians whose goal is to help you understand the context of what you are studying as it relates to the rest of Scripture, God's character, and what the passage means for your life. Of necessity, the commentaries include the author's interpretations. While interesting and helpful, keep in mind that the Commentary is simply one person's understanding of what these passages mean. Other godly men and women have views that are also worth considering.

Pause to contemplate each "Think about" section, marked with the notepad symbol. These features, embedded in the Commentary, offer a place to pause and consider some of the principles being brought out by the text. They provide excellent ideas to journal about or to discuss with other believers, especially those doing the study with you.

Jot down insights or prayer points from the "Personalize this lesson" marked with the ☑ check box symbol. While the "Apply what you have learned" section focuses on doing, the "Personalize this lesson" section focuses on becoming. Spiritual transformation is not just about doing right things and refraining from doing wrong things—it is about changing from the inside out. To be transformed means letting God change our hearts so that our attitudes, emotions, desires, reactions, and goals are increasingly like Jesus'. Often this section will discuss something that you cannot do in your own strength—so your response will usually be something to pray about. Remember that becoming more Christ-like is not just a matter of trying harder—it requires God's empowerment.

Letters to Christians in Crisis
1 and 2 Thessalonians

What will happen when Jesus comes again? Am I ready? What happens to people I love who have already died? What about people who don't know Him? Is it possible that I am already living in the "end times"?

Like many people today, the new believers in Thessalonica had many questions and concerns about the future. They needed reassurance and truth that would give them confidence, even in the midst of difficult and perplexing times.

Paul wrote his first and second letters to the Thessalonians to settle their hearts and minds about these issues, and to encourage them to walk in a manner worthy of Christ that would give them confidence when He returns. His words to them are just as meaningful to us today, as we, like them, wait for that great day.

Some of the themes of 1 and 2 Thessalonians include:

❖ Living to please God

❖ Jesus' second coming

❖ Grieving, but not without hope

❖ Apostasy, rebellion and the "man of lawlessness"

❖ A time of coming judgment

❖ Justice for the persecuted and oppressed

1. What questions or concerns do you have about death or Jesus'
    second coming?

    Why will Jesus allow such horrible times to occur for those he loves?

2. If Jesus were to return or if you were to die this week, is there
    anything you would want to do to prepare? If so, what?

    God is not some big 'thought' in the sky but our creator the giver of life and personal Savior, Jesus, and helper the Holy Spirit

    we need God and we must pay attention.

3. What encouragement would you give to people who are being
    persecuted or oppressed?

    First I cannot begin to understand but know that God allows this for greater glory and walks with them. Also we are a moment You are forever

*If you are doing this study with a group, take time to pray for one another
about your answers to questions 1 and 2. Ask God to reveal truth to you as
you study about these critical matters. If you are studying by yourself, write
your prayer in the blank space below.*

Help me to be pure in heart - clean heart - live, love and work for Jesus.

Lesson 1 Commentary

Letters to Christians in Crisis
1 and 2 Thessalonians

The apostle Paul spread the Christian gospel to Gentiles all over the Roman Empire. In local synagogues, he preached that Jesus was the Jewish Messiah. Some Jews believed Paul's message. Others became his bitter enemies, pursuing him from city to city. Many Gentiles—called "God-fearers"—regularly attended these synagogues, heard and accepted the gospel message, and led their pagan friends to Christ. New congregations included believing Jews, God-fearers, and ex-pagans. Paul hoped to stay long enough to instruct these young churches in the faith, but was often hauled to court, slapped with trumped-up charges, and forced to leave town. He left concerned about these new congregations. Would the church members be persecuted? Would they be led astray or revert to paganism? He kept in contact with them through letters. Aides like Timothy took Paul's letters to the churches, returning to him with news and any questions from his spiritual children.

[handwritten margin notes: 3 groups, Jews, Gentiles, Pagans]

The City and the Church

Acts 17:1-4 describes the birth of the Thessalonian church. Thessalonica (modern-day Salonika) was the capital of Macedonia (northern Greece). Repopulated about 315 BC by order of King Cassander, this ancient city of 200,000 on the *Via Egnatia* (a major Roman trade route) was a main port on the Aegean Sea. Rome conquered Macedonia in 167 BC. Thessalonica teemed with Greeks, Asians, Romans, and Jews under Roman rule. Paul debated in the synagogue for three Sabbath days. In that short time new Christians included Jews, devout Greeks (Gentiles), and leading women (Acts 17:4).

Paul's success aroused hostility. Envious Jews incited thugs to mob Jason's home, where Paul spent time. They pressed false charges persuading city officials to penalize Jason, who posted a bond saying Paul would cause no more turmoil. That could be guaranteed only by Paul's departure. But his leaving did not satisfy the opposition. Thessalonian Jews pursued Paul to Berea, forcing him to leave there. The weary apostle moved on to Athens, where Timothy met him before going to Thessalonica to encourage the believers. Timothy learned that Paul's departure caused them great concern.

The Contents of the Letters

Timothy's arrival with news of the church prompted Paul to write to the Thessalonians. They thrived despite persecution and Paul's foes slandering his ministry, but they had concerns about Christ's second coming. In 1 Thessalonians, Paul recounts his ministry to them, discusses *"how you ought to walk, and to please God"* (4:1) and clarifies questions about the second coming. Whoever took the first letter to the Thessalonians must have returned to Corinth with further concerns. Persecution was intense and some Thessalonians thought the dreadful day of the Lord was already upon them. Paul quickly responds to the latest news with a second letter. Again he thanks God for their faith and assures them of Christ's second coming. He calms their fears, explaining that the day of the Lord cannot prevail until an evil figure, *"the man of lawlessness,"* is revealed. He exhorts them to stand firm and concludes with a request for prayer and a warning against idleness.

The letters reflect a theology still very close to traditional Jewish views. These early Christians believed in God the Father and in Jesus Christ as God's Son. They knew He had been killed by His own people, rose from the dead, and would come again. They believed He was the Savior and believed in the Holy Spirit. They accepted as truth the necessity of a holy life, eternal judgment, and the opposition of Satan and the antichrist. From the very beginning these tenets were the basic beliefs of the Christian church.

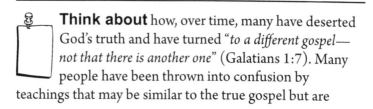

Think about how, over time, many have deserted God's truth and have turned *"to a different gospel— not that there is another one"* (Galatians 1:7). Many people have been thrown into confusion by teachings that may be similar to the true gospel but are misleading in some way. The early Christians believed truth, and truth does not change. What Paul wrote to the Thessalonians is still truth for us.

The Hopes and Habits of Faith Under Fire

To establish the church in Thessalonica, Paul had labored against the city's practices of idolatry and impurity, impressing new converts with his love and dedication. Through sudden and violent circumstances, he was expelled without a chance for "last words" to prepare the new believers to carry on under stressful conditions. Paul writes not as a brilliant rabbi using logic to persuade an audience, but as a missionary and fellow sufferer. He addresses the needs of Christians facing opposition and persecution with warnings, assurance, encouragement, support, and reason to endure. His two main themes are how to live in order to please God, and the return of Jesus Christ.

The Authorship of the Letters

Evidence supports Paul's authorship of these letters and early church tradition confirms it. That both letters begin, "*Paul, Silvanus and Timothy, To the church of the Thessalonians*" suggests Paul's care to present himself in unity with the fellow missionaries he co-labored with. Silvanus (Silas) was a leader of the Jerusalem church. Timothy received the gospel from Paul and became his aide. The theory of co-authorship exists because of verses where Paul breaks the flow of "*we*" to discuss his own thoughts. But the problem of authorship vanishes if we accept that the greeting means what it says. Paul's leadership is clear; but all three men banished from Thessalonica prayed for and communicated with the believers they had left behind.

Personalize this lesson.

☑ Paul was concerned for the new believers at Thessalonica. They had just come out of paganism, and now they faced persecution. They were vulnerable spiritually and otherwise. So, Paul prayed for them, encouraged them, instructed them, warned them, sent Timothy to come alongside them.

Do you know anyone who is spiritually vulnerable—either someone you know personally, or perhaps a person or group of people you have heard about? Ask God if there is a way for you to be involved with them.

A Man of Integrity
1 Thessalonians 1:1-2:16

❖ **1 Thessalonians 1:2-10—The Definition of a Believer**

1. What are the reasons Paul thanks God for the Thessalonians? (1:3)

   work prompt'd by faith
   labor - by love
   endurance - by hope

2. What are the signs of true conversion found in 1:4-10?

   gospel came with words and
   with power from the Holy Spirit
   and with deep conviction

3. How does the end of verse 5 prepare the way for verse 6?

   Paul etc lived among them - they
   saw and became imitators

4. How does verse 6 specifically challenge your behavior or thoughts?

   in spite of severe suffering
   to welcome the message
   with joy from the Holy
   Spirit

❖ 1 Thessalonians 2:1-6—A Model of Ministry

5. What charges implied in these verses have been brought against Paul and his coworkers?

    error

    impure motives

    trickery

6. Which phrase would you choose from this passage to best represent the major requirement of one who witnesses for God? Explain.

    not trying to please men but please God

    keeps us on point

❖ 1 Thessalonians 2:6-9—A Style of Ministry

7. What qualities do you see in Paul that you appreciate?

    integrity

    perseverence

    gentleness

8. How can you see this style of ministry being effective?

    Shared lives with them as well as the gospel. Would help seen as people

❖ 1 Thessalonians 2:10-12—Characteristics of a Christian Witness

9. Using a dictionary, define these words.

    a. *holy* _____

    _____

    b. *righteous* _____

    _____

c.   *blameless* _____

_____

10. How does the cause of Christ and His church suffer when these qualities are absent from those who claim to represent Him?

people are hyprocricy

_____

11. What approach does Paul take toward being a Christian witness and minister in verses 7-12?

gentleness
transparency
worked for their own keep so not do
be a burden

12. What does the phrase *"each one of you"* (2:12) imply about Paul's work among the Thessalonians?

personally interested in each one
individual

_____

❖ 1 Thessalonians 2:13-16—The Apostle's Thanksgiving to God

13. Why did Paul thank God constantly?

They received word of God as word
of God and this worked in them
(was at work)

14. Paul suggests two different ways of responding to the Word of God. What are they and how might they relate to you?

could be seen as word from men
or word from God.
word from men is interesting
word from God is absolute, true
pure, powerful etc

15. How might hearing about the Judean church encourage the
    Thessalonians in their suffering?

*realized that they were not
alone in suffering for Christ*

Apply what you have learned. Paul tenderly
writes about how he, Silvanus, and Timothy led
the Thessalonians to faith in the gospel despite the
opposition. They appealed to them with the gentleness of a
loving mother and the urging of an encouraging father. Through
their approach, the Thessalonians received and accepted the
word of God. Reflect on the people in your life who need the
truth and encouragement of the gospel. In what specific ways
can you take on Paul's example in appealing to them?

A Man of Integrity
1 Thessalonians 1:1-2:16

In chapters 1 and 2, Paul reminds the Thessalonians of their conversion and his ministry to them. Gentiles as well as Jews persecuted them. Those who instigated Paul's expulsion tried to weaken his ministry by destroying his reputation, saying he deceived people, taught a false faith, and wanted his converts' money. Daily attacks against their faith could wear down these new Christians. Paul tries to banish their doubts, reminding them of God's power at their conversion and stating how he and other apostles had behaved among them.

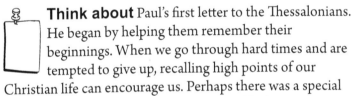

Think about Paul's first letter to the Thessalonians. He began by helping them remember their beginnings. When we go through hard times and are tempted to give up, recalling high points of our Christian life can encourage us. Perhaps there was a special time when you sensed God's presence and help. Remembering God's faithfulness from your past can encourage you now in a difficult time.

Greeting and Thanksgiving

Only in this letter does Paul use the phrase "*the church ... in God*" (1:1), qualifying "*church*" because the word meant any sort of *assembly*. When acknowledging the presence of associates in his greeting, Paul usually moves straight to the first-person pronoun "I." But here, the greeting and thanksgiving include Paul, Silvanus (Silas), and Timothy.

Faith, hope, and *love* often join hands in Paul's letters. In the New

Testament, faith usually refers to a demonstrated trust in Jesus Christ. According to the Bible, the devil and his demons believe God exists and that Jesus Christ is His Son. But the devil lacks trust in Christ as his Lord and Savior (James 2:19). Christian faith goes far beyond mere intellectual agreement to Christian truth; it involves decision and conduct. True faith results in obedience to God that produces changes in one's behavior.

The Thessalonians' living faith and Christian love prompted them to labor hard on Christ's behalf. They ministered to each other gladly because love motivated them, and they were steadfast because of hope. Biblical hope believes that God will do as He promised. The Thessalonians expected Christ's victorious return to rescue them *"from the wrath to come"* (1:10). Paul reminds the Thessalonians that God *"has chosen you"* (1:4), proving it with three points. First, the gospel with the Holy Spirit's help caused them to believe. Second, the Holy Spirit was active in those who proclaimed the message and in those who received it. Third, God planted a deep inner persuasion. Despite severe suffering, they received the message of grace with joy and spread that message; news of their faith in God spread. Christianity demands not only to be broadcast, but also to be modeled as it obviously was here.

The Thessalonians turned from *idols* (Greek *eidolon, image*) to serve the living and true God, hoping Christ's return would occur in their lifetime. Jesus, who Paul significantly refers to as the Son of God in these letters, left heaven once and will leave again to claim victory over Satan's power and to establish His kingdom and glory forever. Through their authentic, vibrant lifestyle, the Thessalonians demonstrated that they were God's people.

In chapter 2, Paul defends his and his companions' effort: They brought them the message despite persecution; their motives were pure; and they were trying to please God, not men. Because the Greek world was overrun with charlatans, it was vital to assure new Christians that the message and the messengers were pure, and the gospel unpolluted. Paul, Silas, and Timothy did not *"deceive"* them. Nor did they use *"words of flattery."* Instead, Paul and his fellow workers spoke as men *"approved by God"* (2:4), who sought to please God alone.

Pseudo-philosophers and religious teachers wandered the Roman Empire, using false teaching, deception, flattery, and occult power to gain a following. Paul separates himself and his ministry from such men by recording his high sense of responsibility and steadfast obedience to God's call; he is willing to suffer for the sake of the gospel—even to death.

Paul's Previous Ministry to the Thessalonians

Paul's team members work hard to provide for themselves, offending the Roman world that disdained manual labor. Paul could have argued that according to Christian custom the Thessalonians had to support him (see 1 Corinthians 9). But he refused financial aid, perhaps because his enemies looked for any reason to accuse him. After a church was established he sometimes accepted their aid, but never required it, proving his financial integrity. The team works in a *"holy and righteous and blameless"* way (1 Thessalonians 2:10), like fathers who encourage and exhort; earlier Paul said they were like nursing mothers. These images convey the many sides of "spiritual parenting." At times people need gentleness like that of a mother with a child; at other times they need a father's exhortation and encouragement.

The Thessalonians received the gospel as God's truth despite the trouble it would bring them. Paul says they share the kind of persecution endured earlier by Judea's Jewish believers. He talks of two parties among the Jews of Jerusalem: those who believe the gospel, and those who persecute the believers. These Jews crucified Jesus and then afflicted the Jerusalem church.

All must face God's judgment, but those who *"displease God and oppose all mankind"* (2:15) will be condemned. They not only personally reject Christ, but try to rid the world of believers. God's wrath differs from human wrath. It is not a loss of temper, but a holy attitude against sin and evil, particularly the evil of opposing the gracious work of salvation. God's *"wrath has come upon them at last"* (1 Thessalonians 2:16). The Greek, *eis telos*, suggests *completeness, fulfilled purpose*. God can and will use any and everything as He moves toward the establishment of His kingdom and the end of all those who have come against it.

Personalize this lesson.

☑ Paul's unidentified critics accused him of people-pleasing, money grubbing, and bad theology, among other things. He welcomed an investigation of his life and the lives of his fellow workers. Paul's transparent integrity reinforced the message he shared. Paul modeled the attributes of love and faithfulness. He earned the right to instruct and challenge. None of the claims people brought against him stuck because he lived what he believed and thought.

What areas of your life are closely aligned to what you say and believe? Are there areas that need to come into alignment? Talk with God about these areas. He welcomes such a conversation and wants to help.

Lesson 3

A Pastor's Concern
1 Thessalonians 2:17–4:12

Memorize God's Word: 1 Thessalonians 4:7-8.

❖ **1 Thessalonians 2:17–3:3—Paul Longs to See Them**

1. What motivated Paul's ministry to the Thessalonians? How does this challenge you?

No one would be unsettled by trials

strengthen + encourage them in their faith, knowing they would be persecuted. Their faith is they are their hope joy glory crown when Jesus comes.

2. What kept Paul from returning to Thessalonica?

satan

3. What do you do when you encounter a "closed door"?

usually take it to man God doesn't want me to go through it – trust.

4. The Thessalonians had already received the Word of God. Why was it so imperative to Paul to work with them further?

strengthen them in their faith encourage them in midst of trials Keep them from doubt and discouragement.

5. What was to be Timothy's role?

   spreading the gospel
   Strengthen + encourage

6. How might knowing that Christians are destined to affliction keep them from being moved by these troubles?

   understand they are not
   the only ones. Helps to stand
   firm.

❖ **1 Thessalonians 3:4-10—Paul's Concern for Them**

7. What does Paul fear has happened?

   They had been tempted by tempter

8. What does 3:10 suggest as the reason for Paul's fear concerning the Thessalonians?

   fill what is lacking in their faith

9. What brought comfort to Paul in his distress?

   Timothy brought news of their
   faith + love

10. What did Paul pray night and day concerning the Thessalonians?

    he would see them again

11. What example do you have in your life of this type of praying?

    Deb.

❖ 1 Thessalonians 3:11-13—Paul's Prayer for Them

12. What does Paul pray for the Thessalonians?

to live holy life
avoid sexual immorality
quiet life work w your own hands so daily
life will win the respect of others

13. Are you surprised that Paul does not pray for persecution to cease? Why, or why not?

why does he not pray for this ??

14. How does Paul's example inspire you?

stay the course
love
encourage
strengthen others

❖ 1 Thessalonians 4:1-8—Living to Please God

15. According to these verses, what does a life pleasing to God look like?

Sanctification, purity
Brotherly love
Quiet life   mind your own business
Work.

16. Paul suggests that *"passion of lust"* causes a person to *"wrong his brother."* What do you think he means by this?

go after another's wife
or brother is influenced badly
by lustful behavior

❖ 1 Thessalonians 4:9-12—Faith's Evidence

17. If the Thessalonians already love *"all the brothers throughout Macedonia,"* why do you think Paul said, *"do this more and more"*?

   so others would see
   so everyone who would know

18. What does 4:11-12 imply about at least some members of this young church?

   some must be nosy
   busibodies

19. What are the two reasons for Paul's instructions in 4:11-12?

   win respect of outsiders
   not be dependent on others

20. Why is Paul concerned with what outsiders would think about the behavior of God's people?

   so they would be
   ready to listen

Apply what you have learned. There is sometimes a tendency to elevate faith to an ethereal level where few Christians can manage to breathe! Here we have seen faith on the ground of everyday life where it belongs. Faith is the shared hard work of loving and wondering and waiting and winning respect. It is also the gift of God (Ephesians 2:8), tended and galvanized by His faithful intervention. Two truths stand in tension, peacefully coexisting. Faith is work and faith is a gift. Neither aspect is complete without the other. In what practical ways are you working out the gift of faith that God has given you?

A Pastor's Concern
1 Thessalonians 2:17–4:12

In the opening paragraphs of this letter, Paul reassured the Thessalonians that their faith is genuine and his apostolic ministry is authentic. The backdrop is an anti-Christian element that said Paul was in the ministry for his own gain. Perhaps Paul's enemies told the Thessalonians that he had forgotten them and moved to a place of greater financial reward. In any case, Paul assures the Thessalonians of his loyalty, explains why he has not returned to them, and expresses his joy over their progress as reported by Timothy. This passage reveals the deep commitment Paul and his converts have to each other.

Paul Desires to See Them (1 Thessalonians 2:17–3:5)

Forced by persecution to leave the young Thessalonian church, Paul describes his departure as being *"torn away"* (1 Thessalonians 2:17). What may have stopped Paul from returning to Thessalonica was the awareness that his enemies were watching for him and would incite another riot if he came back. He was concerned that the church leaders would lose the bond money they had put down for him, and persecution of the church would get worse. Satan lurked behind these obstacles: *"We wanted to come to you—I, Paul, again and again—but Satan hindered us"* (2:18).

Because Paul was prevented from seeing these believers, he sent *"Timothy ... to establish and exhort"* them in their faith (3:2). Persecution targeted Paul so Timothy could slip back into Thessalonica unnoticed. Paul was concerned that these young, persecuted converts might not be able to stand firm in the face of opposition. If they did give up, they would cease to be a vital witness for Christ, the church would die, and the message of grace would vanish from Thessalonica. This is probably what Paul means by *"our labor would be in vain"* (3:5). He sees Satan (*"the tempter"*) as the one who would discourage the Thessalonians. Leading up to this statement, verses 3-4 emphasize that the Thessalonian believers should not *"be moved by these afflictions … For when we were with you, we kept telling you beforehand that we were to suffer affliction."*

Paul's Joy Over Timothy's Report (1 Thessalonians 3:6-13)

Timothy's report that the Thessalonians *"remember* [them] *kindly and long to see* [them]*"* (3:6) greatly encourages the apostle. Paul writes, *"We pray most earnestly night and day that we may see you face to face"* (3:10). Then the purpose and tone of his prayer changes: *"May our God and Father Himself, and our Lord Jesus, direct our way to you."* Interestingly, even though the subject is plural, the Greek word for *"direct our way"* is singular. Paul underlines the oneness between God and Jesus, the mystery of the Trinity.

Paul prays that the Thessalonians' love will *"increase and abound"* (3:12), and that the Lord may strengthen their hearts, so they will be *"blameless in holiness before our God and Father, at the coming of our Lord Jesus with all His saints"* (3:13). By this he means that when Christ returns, He will find the Thessalonians living godly and authentic lives. This is not a prayer for deliverance from trouble; instead, Paul's concern is love and uprightness between people and before God.

Paul's Exhortation to Holiness (1 Thessalonians 4:1-12)

Paul now looks at the moral outworking of faith. For the first time, the language is authoritative: *"we urge you through the Lord Jesus"* (4:2). Though patient and gentle, Paul and his coworkers also oversee that God's people obey His will. For Christians, morality is not a choice; it is a command.

In the pagan world of the 1st century, extramarital sex for men was the norm. Mistresses and prostitutes were acceptable. To people living in this environment, Paul says: *"This is the will of God … that you abstain from sexual immorality; that each one of you know how to control his own body in holiness and honor, not in the passion of lust like the Gentiles"* (4:3-5). *"This is the will of God"* means *"This is God's gracious design"* for humans. Being holy and honorable with our passions is God's beautiful intent for sexuality. True intimacy and love cannot be found outside His special design for us. Those who relate to others based on lust are missing the blessings of sexual purity. When we *"know God"*—understand His true character and trust that His ways are right—we will gladly avoid the pain of misguided, harmful relationships and activities.

No doubt this passage has a broad scope of immorality in mind. The word for *"wrong his brother"* is a superlative, referring to crossing a forbidden boundary. One scholar interprets it this way: "No one is to enrich himself in this matter at his brother's expense, by taking his wife away." Paul makes clear that this is no mere cultural value: *"Whoever disregards this, disregards not man but God"* (4:8).

Think about how God has good reasons for the restrictions He places on people. His prohibitions promote human dignity and worth and preserve society. Fire brings warmth and benefits society. But when all rules are cast aside about when, where, and how fires can be set, what was meant to be a blessing becomes a curse. Sexual laxity proves this. Because most of us have tasted the bitter fruits of immorality, either through our own sin or the sin of others, we understand the biblical plea for holiness. But we also know that God forgives sin. If punishment is deserved, we should leave that in the hands of God, who is both just and merciful. Our focus must turn to obeying the command to forgive—both ourselves and others.

The conclusion of this passage warns of a second danger. Christians who will not work set a bad example and give a poor witness to the outside world. Paul, Silas, and Timothy served God wholeheartedly and labored with their hands in order to relieve the community of any hardship. Paul's command to them—and to us—is *"to live quietly, to mind your own affairs, and to work with your hands, as we instructed you, so that you may walk properly before outsiders and be dependent on no one"* (4:11-12).

Personalize this lesson.

How deeply Paul loved his converts, and they loved him! The Bible pictures believers as a spiritual family—brothers, sisters, parents, and children devoted to each other. Do you love your spiritual family and long to spend quality time with them? Or is Christian fellowship on the fringes of your life? Consider Jesus' words, *"By this all people will know that you are My disciples, if you have love for one another"* (John 13:35).

Engaging God's Word

James

Engage Bible Studies

Tools That Transform

Engage Bible Studies

an imprint of

 COMMUNITY BIBLE STUDY

Engaging God's Word: James
Copyright © 2012 by Community Bible Study. All rights reserved.
ISBN 978-1-62194-000-5

Published by Community Bible Study
790 Stout Road
Colorado Springs, CO 80921-3802
1-800-826-4181
www.communitybiblestudy.org

Printed in the United States of America.

Contents

Introduction

Welcome to the life-changing adventure of engaging with God's Word! Whether this is the first time you've opened a Bible or you've studied the Scriptures all your life, good things are in store for you. Studying the Bible is unlike any other kind of study you have ever done. That's because the Word of God is *"living and active"* (Hebrews 4:12) and transcends time and cultures. The earth and heavens as we know them will one day pass away, but God's Word never will (Mark 13:31). It's as relevant to your life today as it was to the people who wrote it down centuries ago. And the fact that God's Word is living and active means that reading God's Word is always meant to be a personal experience. God's Word is not just dead words on a page—it is page after page of living, powerful words—so get ready, because the time you spend studying the Bible in this *Engaging God's Word* course will be life-transforming!

Why Study the Bible?

Some Christians read the Bible because they know they're supposed to. It's a good thing to do, and God expects it. And all that's true! However, there are many additional reasons to study God's Word. Here are just some of them.

We get to know God through His Word. Our God is a relational God who knows us and wants us to know Him. The Scriptures, which He authored, reveal much about Him: how He thinks and feels, what His purposes are, what He thinks about us, how He views the world He made, what He has planned for the future. The Bible shows us God's many attributes—His kindness, goodness, justice, love, faithfulness, mercy, compassion, creativity, redemption, sovereignty, and so on. As we get to know Him through His Word, we come to love and trust Him.

God speaks to us through His Word. One of the primary ways God speaks to us is through His written Word. Don't be surprised if, as you read the Bible, certain parts nearly jump off the page at you, almost as if they'd been written with you in mind. God is the Author of this incredible book, so that's not just possible, it's likely! Whether it is to find comfort, warning, correction, teaching, or guidance, always approach God's Word with your spiritual ears open (Isaiah 55:3) because God, your loving heavenly Father, has things He wants to say to you.

God's Word brings life. Just about everyone wants to learn the secret to "the good life." And the good news is, that secret is found in God's Word. Don't think of the Bible as a bunch of rules. Viewing it with that mindset is a distortion. God gave us His Word because as our Creator and the Creator of the universe, He alone knows how life was meant to work. He knows that love makes us happier than hate, that generosity brings more joy than greed, and that integrity allows us to rest more peacefully at night than deception does. God's ways are not always "easiest" but they are the way to life. As the Psalmist says, *"If Your law had not been my delight, I would have perished in my affliction. I will never forget Your precepts, for by them You have given me life"* (Psalm 119:92-93).

God's Word offers stability in an unstable world. Truth is an ever-changing negotiable for many people in our culture today. But building your life on constantly changing "truth" is like building your house on shifting sand. God's Word, like God Himself, never changes. What He says was true yesterday, is true today, and will still be true a billion years from now. Jesus said, *"Everyone then who hears these words of Mine and does them will be like a wise man who built his house on the rock"* (Matthew 7:24).

God's Word helps us to pray effectively. When we read God's Word and get to know what He is really like, we understand better how to pray. God answers prayers that are according to His will. We discover His will by reading the Bible. First John 5:14-15 tells us that *"this is the confidence that we have toward Him, that if we ask anything according to His will He hears us. And if we know that He hears us in whatever we ask, we know that we have the requests that we have asked of Him."*

How to Get the Most out of *Engaging God's Word*

Each *Engaging God's Word* study contains key elements that have been carefully designed to help you get the most out of your time in God's Word. Slightly modified for your study-at-home success, this approach is very similar to the tried-and-proven Bible study method that Community Bible Study has used with thousands of men, women, and children across the United States and around the world for nearly 40 years. There are some basic things you can expect to find in each course in this series.

- ❖ Lesson 1 provides an overview of the Bible book (or books) you will study and questions to help you focus, anticipate, and pray about what you will be learning.

- ❖ Every lesson contains questions to answer on your own, commentary that reviews and clarifies the passage, and three special sections called "Apply what you have learned," "Think about" and "Personalize this lesson."

- ❖ Some lessons contain memory verse suggestions.

Whether you plan to use *Engaging God's Word* on your own or with a group, here are some suggestions that will help you enjoy and receive the most benefit from your study.

Spread out each lesson over several days. Your *Engaging God's Word* lessons were designed to take a week to complete. Spreading out your study rather than doing it all at once allows time for the things God is teaching you to sink in and for you to practice applying them.

Pray each time you read God's Word. The Bible is a book unlike any other because God Himself inspired it. The same Spirit who inspired the human authors who wrote it will help you to understand and apply it if you ask Him to. So make it a practice to ask Him to make His Word come alive to you every time you read it.

Read the whole passage covered in the lesson. Before plunging into the questions, take time to read the specific chapter or verses that will be covered in that lesson. Doing this will give you important context for the whole lesson. Reading the Bible in context is an important principle in interpreting it accurately.

Begin learning the memory verse. Learning Scripture by heart requires discipline, but the rewards far outweigh the effort. Memorizing a verse allows you to recall it whenever you need it—for personal encouragement and direction, or to share with someone else. Consider writing the verse on a sticky note or index card that you can post where you will see it often or carry with you to review during the day. Reading and re-reading the verse often—out loud when possible—is a simple way to commit it to memory.

Re-read the passage for each section of questions. Each lesson is divided into sections so that you study one small part of Scripture at a time. Before attempting to answer the questions, review the verses that the questions will cover.

Answer the questions without consulting the Commentary or other reference materials. There is great joy in having the Holy Spirit teach you God's Word on your own, without the help of outside resources. Don't cheat yourself of the delight of discovery by reading the Commentary prematurely. Wait until after you've completed the lesson.

Repeat the process for all the question sections.

Prayerfully consider the "Apply what you have learned," marked with the 📌 push pin symbol. The vision of Community Bible Study is not to just gain knowledge about the Bible, but to be transformed by it. For this reason, each set of questions closes with a section that encourages you to apply what you are learning. Usually this section involves action—something for you to do. As you practice these suggestions, your life will change.

Read the Commentary. *Engaging God's Word* commentaries are written by theologians whose goal is to help you understand the context of what you are studying as it relates to the rest of Scripture, God's character, and what the passage means for your life. Of necessity, the commentaries include the author's interpretations. While interesting and helpful, keep in mind that the Commentary is simply one person's understanding of what these passages mean. Other godly men and women have views that are also worth considering.

Pause to contemplate each "Think about" section, marked with the notepad symbol. These features, embedded in the Commentary, offer a place to pause and consider some of the principles being brought out by the text. They provide excellent ideas to journal about or to discuss with other believers, especially those doing the study with you.

Jot down insights or prayer points from the "Personalize this lesson" marked with the ☑ check box symbol. While the "Apply what you have learned" section focuses on doing, the "Personalize this lesson" section focuses on becoming. Spiritual transformation is not just about doing right things and refraining from doing wrong things—it is about changing from the inside out. To be transformed means letting God change our hearts so that our attitudes, emotions, desires, reactions, and goals are increasingly like Jesus'. Often this section will discuss something that you cannot do in your own strength—so your response will usually be something to pray about. Remember that becoming more Christ-like is not just a matter of trying harder—it requires God's empowerment.

Lesson 1

Faith and Action
James 1:1

Faith in God means more than a ticket to heaven when we die—it means a changed life, now, this side of eternity. It means more than simply believing good theology and doctrine—it means living in wisdom and integrity, kindness, patience, and generosity, as Jesus did. In this short, practical book, James challenges his readers to live the life that Jesus called them to, not just to think about it or talk about it, but to do it. This, James said, is the evidence of our faith.

Themes you'll encounter in James include:

❖ The spiritual benefit of trials

❖ The characteristics of true wisdom

❖ The necessity of putting God's Word into practice

❖ The importance of caring for the poor

❖ The destructive power of the tongue

❖ The value of prayer

1. Which of the themes you just read about seems most relevant to where you are in your life with God currently? Why?

_____

_____

_____

_____

_____

2. How would you evaluate your experience of prayer at this point
    in your spiritual journey?

    _____

    _____

    _____

    _____

    _____

3. What do you hope God will do for you in the course of this
    Bible study?

    _____

    _____

    _____

    _____

    _____

*Take a few minutes to silently consider the quality of your faith and how it
is evidenced in your life. How would you like to grow your ability to live out
your faith? Ask God for His help—He is more than pleased to give it! If you
are studying with a group, share your thoughts with the group members and
pray for one another. Then check back at the end of the study to celebrate the
transformation that His Spirit has brought in you.*

Faith and Action
James 1:1

The letters to the early church in the New Testament speak to every age, because they give practical teaching on living the Christian life. We struggle to incorporate the words of Jesus into our daily lives, just as the early Christians did. There are many parallels between our age and that of the early church. Then, the Roman Empire was at its peak, but beginning its long and gradual decline. The spirit of the age was one of cynicism. Ethics and morality were at low ebb. We see the same attitudes and actions in the world today. Yet God calls us to live as faithful followers of Jesus Christ.

The epistle of James may be the earliest of the New Testament writings, with the possible exception of Galatians. Written specifically to Christian people in the 1st century, its message has universal application. James is classified as one of the "general epistles," which means it is not addressed to a particular church or person, but to a general audience. It is a collection of useful instructions written to all God's people, scattered throughout the world.

This book addresses the fact that Christianity requires ethical and practical behavior. James urges those who claim to believe in Jesus Christ to translate that belief into constructive action. He speaks of controlling the tongue, caring for the needy, and living a righteous life. He clearly states that problems and pain are essential to growth and to Christian maturity and should be considered beneficial instead of something to be avoided.

The Author of the Letter

Two of the Gospel writers, Mark and Matthew, introduced James as one of the brothers of Jesus (Matthew 13:55; Mark 6:3). The apostle Paul mentioned James, *"the Lord's brother,"* in Galatians 1:19, referring to him as an *"apostle."* He could not have been James the brother of John because, while this letter was written about AD 50, John's brother was martyred by Herod Agrippa in AD 44. What a change had occurred in James' life! He and the Lord's other brothers were obvious skeptics during Jesus' lifetime concerning His Messianic role. This fact witnesses to the reality of the Resurrection and Ascension because these same men *"joined together constantly in prayer"* (Acts 1:14) in Jerusalem with the other disciples as they waited for the Holy Spirit to come.

Although he had previously joined forces with unbelievers in opposing Jesus' ministry, James became deeply involved in the church in Jerusalem. Paul, in his letter to the Corinthians, recognized James in his distinguished and authoritative position as the leader of the Jerusalem church. In this letter, James writes in the form of a typical Jewish sermon, or homily. Whoever took down James' words did so in excellent classical Greek, while the thought and form of the letter are Jewish.

The Content of the Letter

James is considered to be the "Proverbs of the New Testament." Like its Old Testament counterpart, James contains short, incisive statements. It is not a great doctrinal treatise: Jesus' name appears only twice. It does not mention the Cross or the Resurrection or the Holy Spirit. What it does proclaim are the practical, ethical requirements of true faith. James warns people who say they have faith to translate that intellectual assent into action. The seeming conflict between James' emphasis on the necessity of deeds to match one's faith and Paul's teaching that salvation comes through faith and not by works vanishes as we read their writings carefully.

Think about how the message of James is particularly relevant for believers who live in an age that confuses freedom and license because it emphasizes the need to obey God's standards of righteousness. For many who have adopted the world's value system and moral code and allow others to determine their behavior, James is hard reading. The fact that our conduct should be consistent with our profession of faith is stressed repeatedly. In fact, James makes it clear that if there is no outward expression of the faith we say we possess, our faith may not be true faith at all. Let us pray that we will be stimulated to examine ourselves and challenged to change as we consider the things we read in this confrontational little book.

This book was completed between AD 44 (the year James became the leader of the Jerusalem church) and AD 62. According to tradition, AD 62 is the year of James' martyrdom.

James speaks of the importance of putting faith into practice in our everyday lives, a problem which persists to this very day. Actions do speak louder than words! Are we really better able to cope because of our faith? Are we more concerned for those who suffer? Christians who are different, better, more loving because of what they believe are living proof of the existence of God and of His concern for the world He created. The problems were many—persecution, which tested faith severely; snobbery, which led to distinctions between rich and poor, educated and uneducated. There were also troublesome reports that some Jewish believers were priding themselves on their faith while living contradictory lives. There were whispers of quarrels and vicious talk, of Christians despising and judging one another.

As Jesus did, James followed the rabbinic style of using illustrations from everyday life to make his points—small bits which can control and guide horses, rudders which steer large ships, small sparks that ignite a forest, the foolishness of thinking fresh and salt water could come from the same source, or that a fig tree could bear olives. The vocabulary is rich, containing some 70 words not found elsewhere in the Bible. James refers to 21 Old Testament books and obviously knew Jesus' teachings well.

Personalize this lesson.

☑ James' advice regarding quarrels within the Christian community and the sin of judging one another tells us that the early church was not perfect, just as the church today is not perfect. His concluding advice about patience and suffering, the avoidance of making oaths, and the prayer of faith are as contemporary as though they were written today. As you read the introduction and overview of the book, did the Holy Spirit draw your attention to anything that seems especially relevant to you, personally? Talk to God how you'd like for Him to transform you (and perhaps your church) as you study and pray your way through this book.

Faith and Life
James 1:2-27

❖ **James 1:2-8—Tests for Believers**

1. Using a dictionary, define *steadfast* as it relates to the testing of our faith.

    _____

    _____

2. How can steadfastness produce joy in a believer's heart? (See also Romans 5:1-5.)

    _____

    _____

    _____

3. How do believers receive wisdom?

    _____

    _____

    _____

4. How does godly wisdom differ from human or worldly wisdom?

    _____

    _____

    _____

    _____

❖ James 1:9-15—The Origin of Testing

5. How has a Christian who is poor in worldly goods achieved true wealth in Christ?

    _____

    _____

6. What is the proper response to being "lowly"?

    _____

    _____

7. On the other hand, what should be the attitude of wealthy Christians? Why?

    _____

    _____

8. Record the beneficial results of resisting temptation (1:12).

    _____

    _____

    _____

9. In your own words, describe the downward spiral of temptation (1:14-15).

    _____

    _____

    _____

    _____

10. Recall a specific time when you either yielded to or resisted temptation. Can you describe your experience in a way that confirms the truth of verses 9-15?

    _____

    _____

    _____

    _____

❖ James 1:16-18—God's Gifts

11. What did God the Father chose to do *"of His own will"*? (See also 1 Peter 1:22-25.)

_____

_____

_____

12. Who is *"the word of Truth"*? (See also John 1:1, 12.)

_____

13. Explain the relationship of hearing the Word of God to salvation. (See also Romans 10:17.)

_____

_____

_____

_____

❖ James 1:19-21—Our Responses

14. What attitudes and actions are mentioned in these verses?

_____

_____

_____

_____

15. What are we to be quick to do and slow to do? Why are these responses important?

_____

_____

_____

_____

❖ James 1:22-27—Listening and Obeying

16. Explain how a person who only *hears* the Word indulges in self-deception.

17. Describe how a doer of the Word treats the Word.

18. What is the promised result?

19. What three things does James list as outward expressions of religion that has real worth (1:26-27)?

20. Give an example of how the world can stain a Christian (1:27).

Apply what you have learned. What specific challenge to obedience have you personally heard this week as you have listened to God speak through His Word? For many of us, learning to discipline our speech and anger may be a priority. Let Psalm 141:3 be your prayer this week: *"Set a guard, O Lord, over my mouth; keep watch over the door of my lips!"*

Faith and Life
James 1:2-27

The book of James has been called a series of short sermons or a collection of sermon notes. In five chapters, the author introduces a great variety of subjects. Although the style can be abrupt, it is never dull. The rich vocabulary, the illuminating illustrations, the appeal to action all whet our appetite to read further.

In studying his epistle, we find James to be a teacher with integrity. He acknowledges the fact that the people to whom he writes are hurting. God's people live in an ungodly world. They have problems caused by an unfriendly environment. However, the writer does not see that as a negative. Instead, he encourages them that their pain, with God's help, can produce positive results. *"Count it all joy, my brothers, when you meet trials of various kinds, for you know that the testing of your faith produces steadfastness"* (1:2-3).

Trials and Building Human Character

As our wise and loving Father, God permits testings to come our way so that through these experiences we may grow strong and mature in our faith in Jesus. The word *trials* (Greek: *peirasmoi*) has the double sense of outward tests and inward temptations. Thus the varieties of testings for the Christian are very great. So is the grace of God! To benefit from trials, the Christian must learn to depend upon God's strength in time of trouble and to rely on the Holy Spirit to overcome temptations, because God does not tempt anyone. This process will result in maturity in Christ.

Think about how New Testament writers agree that believers are not exempt from trouble. Jesus Himself said, *"In the world you will have tribulation"* (John 16:33). But He also said that He has overcome the world and that He would send His Spirit to help us to be overcomers. Paul encouraged the Romans in his letter to them by insisting that *anything* that God allows in our lives, He can use for good (Romans 8:28-29). Trials help us make progress toward God's goal of our being conformed to the image of His Son. It is *because of* the problems, not *in spite of* them, that we mature. Christians are to be optimistic—regardless of the condition of the world!

One of the greatest needs that struggling Christians face is the need for godly wisdom. In James 1:5, James offers aid: *"If any of you lacks wisdom, let him ask God ... and it will be given to him."* In the Old Testament, *wisdom* is equated with *understanding, comprehension, insight,* and *foresight*. In the mind of James, a Jewish Christian, wisdom is practical knowledge, the God-given ability to see things as God sees them. This is not worldly wisdom that equips one to earn money or pass tests at school. Rather, it gives us the ability to pass the tests of life; it equips us for life. What a wonderful promise—that we will be able to see things from God's perspective! This wisdom helps us make sense out of the things that happen to us and others. James warns us not to be *"double-minded"* (1:8), trying to make the best of both worlds. Such a person is unsettled and unstable in every part of his or her life.

Riches and Poverty

The teaching on riches and poverty in James' letter is particularly thought-provoking. The lowly brother was to *"boast in his high exaltation"* and the rich one *"in his humiliation"* (1:9). The point is that, in heaven, all believers in Christ are *"fellow citizens with God's people"* (Ephesians 2:19) regardless of what positions they may hold on earth.

Trials and Temptation

James again speaks of testing and temptation and the reward for those who not only endure trials and temptations but remain vigorous, productive, and joyful. The *"crown of life"* will be given to the one who *"perseveres."* He touches on the secret of victory under stress by saying this crown has been promised to *"those who love Him."* Love for God produces a desire to please Him and the strength to do so as trials and tests are encountered.

Faith and Conduct

James eloquently discusses at least three subjects in his appeal for Christians to heed the Word of God. He urges his readers to apply wisdom to their everyday life by being quick to listen to others; by being *"slow to speak"* (speak thoughtfully); and by being *"slow to get angry"* (1:19). The Greek word for *anger* is *orge*, meaning *impulse, indignation,* or *wrath.* Angry outbursts are to be avoided because they are irrational, unreasonable, and do more harm than good. When anger is concerned with self-interests, it is not righteous. When anger is a response to sin, it can sometimes be considered *righteous.* Most of us cannot avoid feeling the emotion of anger from time to time; what is most important is that we do not let that anger cause us to sin. The person controlled by the Spirit of God learns what it means *"to be angry and ... not sin"* (Ephesians 4:26).

The key thought in the final section of chapter 1 is, *"Be doers of the word, and not hearers only"* (1:22). James pleads for Christians to let the Word of God that has been planted within them take root and flourish. By doing so, they can be saved from conformity to the evil world system— and there are blessings in store for those who practice the Word.

James then presents a direct challenge: *"If anyone thinks he is religious and does not bridle his tongue but deceives his heart, this person's religion is worthless"* (1:26). To be truly religious is to be able to master oneself. Because the tongue is so difficult to control, a believer's control of it gives evidence of self-control in all of life. It is a test of true spirituality.

Personalize this lesson.

☑ You and I are called to exercise our faith in Jesus Christ. As the title of this lesson indicates, we are to reflect the reality, vitality, and practicality of our faith in our daily lives. Hearing the Word of God is necessary and important, for our faith begins through hearing. We need to hear God's Word to know His heart and respond to His love toward us. Sadly, if we hear and do not act on what we have heard, our spiritual ears become dull. We learn to tune out our heavenly Father's desires for us when we repeatedly fail to act on them. If, on the other hand, after we have heard, we act, our spiritual hearing grows sharper, we become more mature, and our relationship with the Lord grows! How is your spiritual hearing? What is the last thing God said to you? Are you acting upon it?

Faith and Society
James 2

Memorize God's Word: James 2:8.

❖ James 2:1-7—The Hypocrisy of Favoritism

1. What three words sum up the main thought of this paragraph?

    _____

    _____

2. What is James' practical illustration to help his readers
    understand his point?

    _____

    _____

    _____

3. Besides favoritism toward the wealthy, how else might it be seen
    in the church today?

    _____

    _____

❖ James 2:8-13—The Believer's Relationship to Law

4. Summarize the law pertaining to human relationships in one
    sentence.

    _____

    _____

    _____

5. Why is showing favoritism a violation of this law?

       _____

       _____

6. James 2:13 says, *"Mercy triumphs over judgment."* How has God's mercy saved us from judgment (Romans 8:1-2)?

       _____

       _____

7. Why should we extend mercy to others (Luke 6:35-37; Ephesians 4:32)?

       _____

       _____

❖ James 2:14-19—The Evidence of Faith

Note: For these questions, also read Ephesians 2:8-9.

8. Who is the source and the object of our faith?

       _____

       _____

9. What is the eternal benefit of true faith?

       _____

       _____

10. According to James, how does a believer demonstrate his or her true faith?

       _____

       _____

       _____

11. What two examples does James use for ineffective faith?

       _____

       _____

       _____

12. Comment on your response to his choice of illustrations. How are they relevant today?

_____

_____

_____

❖ James 2:20-23—Proof From Scripture for James' Definition of Faith

13. Read Hebrews 11:17-19, 31. Rewrite James 2:20 as a positive statement rather than a question. (The Greek makes it clear that James meant it to be understood that way.)

_____

_____

_____

14. What two people from Scripture does James cite to illustrate his point about true faith producing results?

_____

_____

15. Read Genesis 22:1-14.

 a. What is the first step through which Abraham is justified (Genesis 15:6)?

_____

_____

 b. Why do you think Abraham's succeeding actions resulted from this first step?

_____

_____

 c. How does the example of Abraham's life challenge you as a believer?

_____

_____

❖ James 2:24-26—An Example of Faith

16. Read Joshua, chapter 2.

   a. Who was Rahab? _____

      _____

   b. How did she give evidence of her faith? _____

      _____

      _____

   c. How was her faith a blessing to her? _____

      _____

      _____

17. Write a short explanation of your understanding of James 2:26.

_____

_____

_____

_____

_____

Apply what you have learned. James says that demons believe that there is only one God, and they *"shudder"* (2:19). However, even their fear does not compel them to honor Him. They are in rebellion against Him and will do anything they can to undermine His purposes and hinder humans from trusting Him. James is pointing out that belief doesn't always lead to love and obedience. We, like the demons, might acknowledge the one true God of the universe, but our actions will show our true attitude toward Him. Have we chosen to love and obey Him, or have we rebelled and refused to let Him "run our lives"? What do your actions say about your response to God and the teachings in His Word? Remember, "Truth not applied is truth denied."

Faith and Society
James 2

A careful study of Scripture will reveal the basic truth that Jesus' primary concern was for the life that lasts forever rather than for the one that is temporal. His desire was to minister to people's spiritual poverty, blindness, and bondage. Jesus consistently identified Himself with society's poor and outcasts. The Old Testament prophets made it clear that when Messiah came He would bring good news to the poor, restore the sight to the blind, set free the oppressed, and heal the brokenhearted.

Discrimination Versus Impartiality

James is concerned that some 1st century Christians are not ministering as Jesus had done to the physically needy in their society. He challenges those who practice discrimination in the church, accusing them of creating distinctions among their fellow Christians. He condemns them for making judgments based on evil motives. He reminds them of God's sovereign grace toward the poor—that God has chosen them to be rich in faith and to be content in the promise of what lies ahead for them. James' concern is equally relevant today.

The apostle then warns the early Christians to beware of the rich people who exploit some and drag others into court, asking if they realize how hurtful those actions are to the reputations of believers as well as to Jesus. The Bible does not condemn wealth. Many men of God were rich, such as Abraham, Job, Solomon, and Joseph of Arimathea.

 Think about how the Bible obviously does not condemn all wealthy people, nor does it condemn money as intrinsically evil. However, it does warn of the seduction of riches (1 Timothy 6:10). The temptation of financially secure people to trust and serve possessions instead of loving God and people is very real (Matthew 6:33). Paul gave this advice to Timothy, his spiritual son: *"As for the rich in this present age, charge them not to be haughty, nor to set their hopes on the uncertainty of riches, but on God, who richly provides us with everything to enjoy. They are to do good, to be rich in good works, to be generous and ready to share, thus storing up treasure for themselves as a good foundation for the future, so that they may take hold of that which is truly life!"* (1 Timothy 6:17).

In the days when Jesus lived on earth, discrimination existed in many forms. Jews refused to communicate with Samaritans (John 4:7-9). The religious would not associate with the misfits and sinners (Matthew 9:10-11; Luke 18:9-14). The wealthy ignored the pleas and pain of the poor (Luke 16:19-22). It was a challenge for the gospel of Jesus Christ to penetrate the world of Israel. Yet Jesus extended Himself to reach the crowds with His message.

Within a few short years, Jesus' disciples were called Christians, because they lived in a way that distinguished them from the rest of society. The same should be true today: Christians should be "living Bibles." The world ought to be able to learn about God by "reading us like a book." James was challenging his readers to fulfill God's Law to *"love your neighbor as yourself"* (James 2:8). Such love is a witness to an unbelieving world.

Think about how *mercy* is having compassion and a forgiving spirit toward those who are hard to get along with or who offend us. It is not difficult to be merciful to those who acknowledge their problems and seek forgiveness and help. But most of us find it almost impossible (unless we rely on God's help) to be merciful to those who resent or ignore our attempts to give forgiveness and help. We can't force them to accept our mercy—but we can still freely offer it. Isn't this what God has done *for us* and will now do *in us* for others.

Faith and Action

James demonstrates that where loving action is conspicuous by its absence, there is clear proof that real faith is also absent. Notice his words carefully: *"if a man claims to have faith but has no deeds."* This is altogether different from saying, "If a man has faith." Simply professing one's faith but totally lacking any tangible results is worthless. Genuine faith joins a man with Jesus Christ so that his thoughts and actions come under the power of the Holy Spirit. "Words-only faith" has no saving power whatsoever.

To emphasize his point, James presents an illustration of a half-naked and hungry person who asks for help and is dismissed with verbal "blessings" only. What benefit is that? Is Jesus Christ honored?

To those who boast of their doctrine, James bluntly warns that intellectual assent to truth is not enough: "What do you think? Believing that God is One is not sufficient! As a matter of fact, so do the demons believe that! They even demonstrate a more frightened attitude to God than you do. They tremble! But they are not saved!" (2:19, Commentary writer's paraphrase). The demons know who God is, and they fear Him, but they continue in their rebellion. Their actions reveal their rejection of God.

The contrast between a true believer and a "words-only" believer is clear. A genuine disciple of Christ lives according to the teachings of the Master. The other is like a tree that produces many leaves but no fruit. James gives two vivid historical illustrations:

❖ Abraham truly trusted the Lord and was declared righteous when he offered his son Isaac on the altar. His actions gave evidence of his belief for all to see.

❖ In the same manner, Rahab the prostitute was declared righteous because of her daring action when she protected the Israelite spies. She acted upon her faith in spite of the danger involved because she believed in the God of Israel and decided to trust in Him.

Personalize this lesson.

☑   Are certain types of people "invisible" to you? Sadly, it is easy to consider certain groups of people as expendable, as "throwaways" not worthy of our attention or care. Have you ever looked the other way when walking by an elderly, disabled, or needy person? Certainly the problem of caring for the less fortunate is a complex and sometimes overwhelming one. Nevertheless, God has blessed each of us with the ability to do *something*. What people are "invisible" to you? Will you ask God to open your eyes and heart to them? What is one small step you could take toward noticing and reaching out to the disenfranchised around you?

Faith and the Human Tongue
James 3

❖ James 3:1-2—The Responsibility of Teachers

1. Who calls and equips a teacher of God's Word (1 Corinthians 12:28)?

   _____

   _____

2. Why do you think teachers are judged more strictly than other believers?

   _____

   _____

3. Paraphrase what James reminds his readers of in the first part of James 3:2.

   _____

   _____

❖ James 3:3-12—The Importance of the Human Tongue

4. What illustrations does James use to describe *"the tongue"*?

   a. _____

   _____

   b. _____

   _____

c. _____

_____

5. According to 3:6, what does the tongue have the ability to do?

_____

_____

6. What have you found to be a helpful Scripture verse, skill, or personal reminder that has helped you to discipline what comes out of your lips?

_____

_____

_____

❖ James 3:13-15—The Importance of Wisdom

7. How does a wise person's life demonstrate his or her wisdom (3:13)?

_____

_____

8. What attitudes are absent from the life of a wise person (3:14)?

_____

_____

9. How should each person assume responsibility for his or her own heart attitudes, according to Proverbs 4:20-23?

_____

_____

❖ James 3:16-18—The Results of Two Kinds of Wisdom

10. What happens where envy and selfish ambition exist?

_____

_____

11. List the eight positive components of God's wisdom from 3:17.

_____

_____

_____

_____

12. a. Concerning the harvest in 3:18, who is honored in this harvest? (See also John 15:8.)

_____

_____

    b. What is the fruit of this harvest? _____

_____

13. What do Romans 12:18 and Hebrews 12:14 advise believers regarding their role as peacemakers?

_____

_____

_____

❖ Reread James 3—Faith and the Human Tongue

14. a. Read Luke 6:43-45 and note the two natures of trees.

_____

_____

_____

    b. How can you tell the nature of the tree you are looking at?

_____

_____

15. a. How is a person's nature disclosed? _____

_____

    b. What is the fruit, and where does it come from?_____

_____

_____

16. How are your answers above relevant to what James has written

   a. about the tongue? _____

   _____

   _____

   b. about wise and understanding people? _____

   _____

   _____

Apply what you have learned. United States President John Adams once said, "Society's demands for moral authority and character increase as the importance of the position increases." Do you agree? Chapter 3 of James certainly indicates that God has high standards for those who want to be teachers and leaders. The characteristics described in 3:13-18 are a good checklist to measure yourself by as you fulfill the ministry that God has called you to. Reread this section, asking the Holy Spirit to reveal any area where you are lacking in *"wisdom from above"* (3:17).

Faith and the Human Tongue
James 3

What would you consider to be one of the greatest problems Christians encounter in living a godly life? Jesus stated it strongly when He said: *"Hear and understand: it is not what goes into the mouth that defiles a person, but what comes out of the mouth … what comes out of the mouth proceeds from the heart, and this defiles a person"* (Matthew 15:10-11, 18). The problem of the tongue is universal! Just as our actions reveal whether our faith is alive, so our tongues reveal whether our hearts are pure.

Desiring To Be Teachers

James begins chapter 3 with a warning to teachers—those whose tongues produce words that can have a profound eternal effect on others. *Teacher* is a high calling indeed; it is one of the most crucial of the New Testament gifts. Teachers occupied a distinguished position among the early Christians; this is evident at Antioch where the teaching of Paul and Barnabas profoundly affected the believers. These two were commissioned to establish churches in Asia Minor and Europe. The gift of evangelism is not mentioned in this text; rather, persons with the gift of teaching were assigned the responsibility of pioneering the Christian work in a pagan world.

Think about how the position of teaching—the ability to influence others—is as desirable now as it was in James' day. The privilege of teaching carries great responsibility since people in this very visible position will be closely watched and judged by others. James warned teachers to speak carefully, for God Himself will judge those who handle His words wrongly. Because each of

us has some measure of influence on others, James' words to
teachers apply generally: we must share what we know of
God, seeing that our lives match our words.

Notice that James considers himself to be a teacher; he uses the pronoun
"*we*" in 3:1. The warning includes himself. Teachers must teach the truth
and live the truth because so many lives will be affected. God holds
teachers to greater accountability. Because no one is infallible and their
tongues are their tools, teachers must guard the way they use them.
The *"perfect"* or *innocent* person is the one who has his or her tongue
completely under control. In fact, if people can control their tongues,
they should be able to master every other part of their bodies because
the tongue is the hardest to control!

Taming the Tongue

*"We all stumble in many ways, and if anyone does not stumble in what he
says, he is a perfect man, able also to bridle his whole body"* (3:2). James
acknowledges that no one is faultless. At the same time, he points
out what every teacher knows—the importance of the tongue as an
instrument of communication. We all know how easily a slip of the
tongue can occur, and James provides three vivid word pictures to
help us understand the destructive power of the tongue. The tongue's
potential for power in individual lives and in human relationships is out
of proportion to its size. It has immense potential for either useful or
destructive effects on ours and others' lives.

As necessary as it is, the tongue is a key instrument for corruption. James
compares the tongue to a fire. Every form of iniquity in the *world* (all the
evil characteristics of a fallen world that loves evil rather than good—its
greed, its lust, its idolatry) finds expression through the tongue. The
tongue has the power to change *"the entire course of* [a person's] *life"* (3:6).

Where does the tongue obtain its destructive power—its flame?
According to James, it is ignited by hell. In the Greek text, the word is
simply *Gehenna*; in James' day the valley of Hinnom south of Jerusalem
served as an incinerator to burn trash, dead animals, and dead bodies of
criminals. It became a symbol of the place of punishment. Experience
tells us that the atmosphere of hell has been brought into this world by a
sharp, lashing tongue.

Think about such an obvious message. We can either be on fire for the Lord, ignited by the Holy Spirit, or we can be set on fire by hell itself. We cannot be both at the same time. What comes out of our mouths reveals what is going on in our hearts. And the truth is that a battle for control rages there. Because the Spirit of God indwells all Christians, each of us has the opportunity to be increasingly conformed to God's image. Will we victoriously fight the inner battle and use our tongues for praising God and blessing those we love?

The tongue is an untamed beast. People can tame wild beasts but they cannot tame the muscle in their mouths. Behind their teeth lies a deadly poison. How is it that poison and blessing can pour from the same mouth? They *cannot* in nature: the same spring cannot produce both fresh and brackish water nor can a fig tree produce olives. They *should* not in the life of a believer!

True Wisdom

James proposes the solution for an unruly tongue: *"Who is wise and understanding among you? By his good conduct let him show his works in the meekness of wisdom"* (3:13). God has promised to give to those who ask. Wisdom includes understanding. These two qualities working together produce *"good conduct"* (3:13), which abounds with both humility and works that honor Christ. The opposite—*"bitter jealousy and selfish ambition"* (3:14), which are outgrowths of pride—can bring only disorder and every evil practice. They are poison to the human heart. Heaven's wisdom is *"pure, peaceable, gentle, open to reason, full of mercy and good fruits, impartial and sincere"* (3:17). Being filled with this kind of wisdom produces results that are remarkably similar to those that come from being filled with the Holy Spirit, who indwells and inspires believers.

Personalize this lesson.

☑ With what person or in what social setting is your tongue most likely to cause damage? Consider how praying for and concentrating on *"the wisdom from above"* (3:17) could change the way you use your tongue with that person or in that setting. Instead of the harmful things that sometimes come out of your mouth, how could you use your tongue to demonstrate God-given wisdom? Think and pray specifically about this. God can cause your heart to be good soil where good fruits can grow. Why not ask Him to take over your life and produce in you a *"harvest of righteousness"* (3:18)?

Faith and Human Struggle
James 4

Memorize God's Word: James 4:7.

❖ James 4:1-3—Quarrels and Fights

1. What is the root cause of troubled relationships?

    _____

    _____

2. How is answered prayer dependent upon a person's

    a. attitudes and motives? _____

    _____

    _____

    b. commitment to God? (See also 1 John 3:21-22.) _____

    _____

    _____

❖ James 4:4-6—Friendship Considered

3. James states that friendship with the world is enmity with God. What do these Scriptures say about this?

    a. Matthew 6:24 _____

    _____

    b. Ephesians 2:1-5 _____

    _____

4. Why can't believers be true friends of the world?

_____

_____

5. According to James, if you are a true friend of the world, what is your relationship with God?

_____

_____

6. How does God enable His true friends to live in a hostile world?

_____

_____

7. What is the eternal benefit of being a true friend of God (see 1 John 2:17)?

_____

_____

❖ James 4:7-10—Submission and Resistance

8. From this passage and Ephesians 6:10-18, what tactics should a believer use in spiritual warfare?

_____

_____

9. Why is it necessary to prepare for spiritual warfare?

_____

_____

10. Define submission in the context of your relationship with God.

_____

_____

11. How do we submit ourselves to God? (See also Romans 12:1-2.)

_____

_____

12. When we follow the instructions given in this passage, what will be the results?

   a. 4:7 _____

   _____

   b. 4:8 _____

   _____

   c. 4:10 _____

   _____

❖ James 4:11-12—Instructions on Judging

13. What is a person doing who slanders or judges another person?

   _____

   _____

14. What do these passages say about the one Lawgiver and Judge, and the extent of His judgment and rule.

   1) John 5:19-23 _____

   _____

   _____

   2) Romans 14:10-12 _____

   _____

   _____

15. What does the one Lawgiver and Judge have the ability to do (James 4:12)?

   _____

   _____

❖ James 4:13-17—Boasting and Obedience

16. Why is it wrong to boast about our plans for the future?

   _____

   _____

17. What should our attitude be about our plans?

_____

_____

_____

_____

18. James 4:17 describes what is called "the sin of omission." What acts does Jesus describe in Matthew 25:41-45 that people will be judged for?

_____

_____

_____

_____

Apply what you have learned. British Statesman Edmund Burke said, "All that is necessary for evil to triumph is for good men to do nothing." Evil (and Satan) must be actively resisted, or it will take over any earthly territory that is not claimed by Christ and His followers. This is true not only in the world around us, but within our own lives. If we do not submit ourselves to God (James 4:7), the devil will not flee—he will hang around harassing and enticing us. We should not allow ourselves to be complacent regarding evil, *"so that we would not be outwitted by Satan; for we are not ignorant of his designs"* (2 Corinthians 2:11). What area of your life do you need to specifically submit to God? Will you do it as completely as you are able and reclaim that territory for God?

Faith and Human Struggle
James 4

Why War?

James was writing to Christians who were dealing with different issues. Already we have seen that these were Christians who showed favoritism based on wealth; Christians who were sound in their doctrine but weak in their sense of duty; Christians who could not control their tongues; Christians who were presumptuously thrusting themselves into the position of teacher. James ends chapter 3 with the statement that *"a harvest of righteousness is sown in peace by those who make peace."* In chapter 4, he speaks of the sinful condition of the human heart. Chapter 3 ends with words about peace; chapter 4 begins with words about war. First-century Christians faced persecution from nonbelievers. However, James speaks of war going on between believers and within believers. God grieves when believers' fellowship is broken by strife.

Strongly, James points out, *"You desire and do not have, so you murder. You covet and cannot obtain, so you fight and quarrel"* (4:2). The daily news confirms this. People and nations seek to destroy each other because they are selfish and self-centered. The wars in the world as well as the ones in the body of Christ begin with battles in the hearts of men and women. Predictably, such Christians experience no power in prayer! Either they forget to ask, or their motives are selfish. Because they are unresponsive to God, He is unresponsive to them.

 Think about how the Bible contains many promises about prayer; yet sometimes when we pray, nothing seems to happen. When our prayers seem to go unanswered, we often get discouraged and may even stop praying. However, a better response would be to ask God what is hindering our prayers. It might be simply that the timing is not right and He wants us to persevere in prayer (see Luke 18:1-8). It could be that our prayer is not according to His will (see 1 John 5:14-15). Or it could be that we are asking with selfish motives, as James points out in 4:2. At any rate, we can be sure that our heavenly Father longs to answer the requests of His children.

Appeal for Humility

A second cause for warring elements in the church is *"friendship with the world"* (4:4). James calls Christians who adopt the world's philosophy and live by it rather than following God *"adulterous people."* He views worldly minded Christians as committing adultery against Christ, the Bridegroom of the church, just as Israel in the Old Testament committed spiritual adultery against God the Father by following after other gods.

Jesus plainly stated, *"No one can serve two masters, for either he will hate the one and love the other, or he will be devoted to the one and despise the other. You cannot serve God and money"* (Matthew 6:24).

Some scholars interpret James 4:5 to mean that God jealously longs for the response of the spirit which He breathed into man. Other scholars interpret it to say that the Holy Spirit whom God has sent to indwell us jealously yearns for our response to Him. Though the exact interpretation is clouded, the point is clear. Believers are called to cooperate with the constraining love of the Spirit of God. God gives His Spirit by His grace. To resist or grieve Him is to arouse God's intense jealousy, because God desires wholehearted devotion. His jealousy differs from the human variety, because God's jealousy is motivated by His desire for the very best for His people. His concern is not for Himself.

James goes on to point out that God gives *"grace"* to the humble. Why? Because it takes grace for men and women to be able to submit. Arrogant people usually do not know their own condition and need. They think they do not need anything, not realizing that they are actually poor, blind, and naked (Revelation 3:17). A humble spirit draws us to God; pride makes Him our opponent.

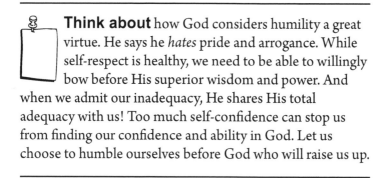 **Think about** how God considers humility a great virtue. He says he *hates* pride and arrogance. While self-respect is healthy, we need to be able to willingly bow before His superior wisdom and power. And when we admit our inadequacy, He shares His total adequacy with us! Too much self-confidence can stop us from finding our confidence and ability in God. Let us choose to humble ourselves before God who will raise us up.

How does James characterize the true, humble child of God? He submits himself to his Maker, who is totally worthy of adoration and submission. He resists the devil by rejecting his plans and standing against him. He draws near to God. Through Jesus Christ, believers have full access into His presence. Our Father delights in having His children draw close to Him in love and prayer. Children of God seek to keep themselves from the pollution and contamination of evil. They know the value of repentance. They mourn when they fail God, unlike those whose self-satisfied joy and laughter show that they do not even realize their failure.

James makes things very clear: *"Humble yourselves before the Lord"* (4:10). To humble yourself means to see yourself as God sees you. The blessings that follow are both immediate and future: grace for the present and the privilege of reigning with Christ in glory in the future.

Appeal for Kindness

James now turns to several other ways Christians assert an arrogant spirit. One manner is to speak evil about others. To do so is to speak against the Law of God, that is, the Law of love. Christians are not called to judge others or the Law. We are saved by God's grace to be doers of the Law of love, not to usurp God's place as Judge.

Warning Against Boasting

It is unwise to make plans for the future, as though we are the final authority over our own lives. James feels compelled to warn people who believe in God—but who apparently live their lives and make their plans without recognizing their dependence upon God and His plans. Should we not plan ahead? Yes. But God wants our planning to be done with *His* will in mind. To recognize God's sovereign grace and power is to maintain a humble posture before Him.

Personalize this lesson.

 The last verse sums up the solution to all the problems James has discussed in chapter 4: *"So whoever knows the right thing to do and fails to do it, for him it is sin"* (verse 17). If you read the Word of God, then there are many things you know to do. What are some of the things God has shown you recently from His Word? Are you doing them? How well do your habits, speech, and attitudes conform to what you read in His Word? We must be careful not to beat ourselves up because we are not perfect. However, we also must not excuse ourselves from moving forward because "we're only human." God shows us a way of living that leads to true life for ourselves and others. He knows that His ways are best for us if only we will learn to walk in them. So while you don't need to eat the whole elephant at once, it is important that you start somewhere. What change is the Holy Spirit specifically calling you to make in your life today? Will you draw near to God so that He can come near to you and work in you to bring about that transformation?

Lesson 6

Faith and Practice
James 5

❖ James 5:1-6—A Warning to the Wealthy

1. Read Matthew 6:19-20. What is the folly of laying up treasures on earth only?

   _____

   _____

2. How did the wealthy people James addresses in this passage support their self-indulgent lifestyle?

   _____

   _____

3. What accusation does James make against wealthy employers in 5:4?

   _____

   _____

4. What warning does Malachi 3:5 give to employers?

   _____

   _____

5. What advice does 1 Peter 5:2-3 give Christians who oversee others?

   _____

   _____

   _____

6. How can a wealthy Christian be a practical blessing to others?

    _____

    _____

    _____

❖ James 5:7-11—The Need for Patience

7. What great hope does James offer to encourage and exhort the believers to be patient?

    _____

    _____

8. How do the following people serve as examples of patience to all believers?

    a. the farmer _____

    _____

    b. the prophets (See also Matthew 5:12.)_____

    _____

    c. Job (See also Job 1:21-22; 42:10.) _____

    _____

❖ James 5:12—The Command Against Oaths

9. Read Matthew 5:34-37. Briefly state what Jesus says about taking oaths.

    _____

    _____

    _____

10. Are there times when it is hard for you to keep the promises you make to others? How do James 5:12 and Matthew 5:34-37 apply to these situations?

    _____

    _____

❖ James 5:13-18—Instructions on Prayer

11. Concerning verse 13, why is it important to pray during times of great stress (Psalm 50:15; Philippians 4:4-7)?

_____

_____

_____

12. How do times of joy offer opportunities for prayer (Colossians 3:15-17)?

_____

_____

_____

13. If a believer is ill and wants prayer, what are the specific steps that may be taken by

a. the sick person? _____

_____

_____

b. the people who pray? _____

_____

_____

c. the Lord? (See also 1 John 5:14.) _____

_____

_____

14. How would you explain the value of confessing sins to one another and praying for one another?

_____

_____

_____

_____

_____

❖ James 5:19-20; Review James 5—Faith and Practice

15. In James' conclusion, what does he say about our responsibility to help restore fellow believers to the truth?

_____

_____

16. If you were telling someone about this chapter, how would you describe

   a. the perils of riches? _____

   _____

   _____

   b. the purpose of patience and steadfastness? _____

   _____

   _____

   c. the power of prayer? _____

   _____

   _____

Apply what you have learned. This chapter seems to be more concerned with attitudes than with actions—our attitudes toward riches we possess; our attitudes toward suffering as we experience it; our attitudes in prayer when we request it for ourselves or offer it for others. Remember, every action is preceded by an attitude. Ultimately you *will* act out in some way how you feel and what you think. Examine your attitudes, and ask the Lord to give you His perspective on them this week.

Faith and Practice
James 5

At first glance, James 5 seems to deal with attitudes toward health and wealth, prayer and pain. And indeed it does. A more careful look reveals repeated references to the Second Coming of Christ. James writes of *"the last days"* (5:3), *"the coming of the Lord"* (5:8), *"the Judge ... at the door"* (5:9). Here at the end of a book dealing with living consistent, concerned lives, James' words remind us that this present evil world is not all there is. His topic is how we should live while we wait for Jesus Christ to return, take control, and make His world right.

Perils of Riches

Verses 1-6 could be titled "The Perils of the Rich," for James challenges the privileged people of his day who were apparently taking advantage of those who are poor and helpless. God never says that it is a sin to be wealthy. The possession of money does not make a man evil any more than the lack of it makes a man virtuous. The pertinent questions are: How was the money acquired? How is it being used?

James accuses those in management of defrauding the poor. The rich are gaining at the expense of the less fortunate But James longs to persuade the rich who are spiritually needy to change their minds and their behavior and so avoid God's judgment.

Patience and Steadfastness

To those who are humiliated and oppressed, James offers words of encouragement in verses 7-12. His advice is presented as four commands:

❖ Be patient! Why? Because God acts at the right time for the right purpose. People tend to act impetuously, regardless of the consequences. Also, patience is a most impressive testimony.

❖ Establish your hearts! Do not become discouraged. Jesus is coming back soon.

❖ Do not grumble! Do not complain against others. The prophets were persecuted, yet remained true to the word of the Lord.

❖ Be true to your word. If you are known for telling the truth and keeping your word, you don't need to make oaths.

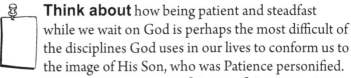

Think about how being patient and steadfast while we wait on God is perhaps the most difficult of the disciplines God uses in our lives to conform us to the image of His Son, who was Patience personified. *"Blessed are all those who wait for* [the Lord]," says Isaiah (30:18). When you wait with hope and trust in the midst of incapacitating troubles, God will replace your weakness with His strength (Isaiah 40:29-31). We must trust in God and claim His coping ability.

The Power of Prayer

As he goes on to give practical advice regarding the power of prayer, James identifies three types of people. His advice to all three is the same: Communicate with God. If we are in distress, pray. God will bring relief either by healing or by giving endurance, patience, or strength to go through the suffering (Isaiah 43:1-2). If we are cheerful, we are to sing praises to God. Rejoice in Him always (Philippians 4:4)! If we are sick, we are to go and tell our spiritual leaders of our condition so that they may minister to our needs. The elders are to do two things: first, anoint with oil, and then, pray.

In the Old Testament, oil symbolized consecration to God. It also spoke of the presence of the Holy Spirit, who comes to empower, energize, and equip those being dedicated. Thus it is appropriate for the spiritual leaders to consecrate the one who suffers to God and ask for a special ministry of the Holy Spirit to that person. Furthermore, since anointing with oil was one of the best known ancient medical practices, many believe its application had both spiritual and physical benefits. James adds another key point: if the one who suffers becomes conscious of sin in his life, he is to confess to God and to other believers in order to receive healing (5:15-16). The implication is that illness is sometimes related to unconfessed sin.

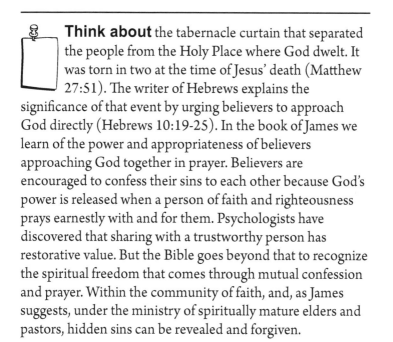

Think about the tabernacle curtain that separated the people from the Holy Place where God dwelt. It was torn in two at the time of Jesus' death (Matthew 27:51). The writer of Hebrews explains the significance of that event by urging believers to approach God directly (Hebrews 10:19-25). In the book of James we learn of the power and appropriateness of believers approaching God together in prayer. Believers are encouraged to confess their sins to each other because God's power is released when a person of faith and righteousness prays earnestly with and for them. Psychologists have discovered that sharing with a trustworthy person has restorative value. But the Bible goes beyond that to recognize the spiritual freedom that comes through mutual confession and prayer. Within the community of faith, and, as James suggests, under the ministry of spiritually mature elders and pastors, hidden sins can be revealed and forgiven.

James exhorts his readers to become praying people. The apostle Paul said, *"Pray without ceasing"* (1 Thessalonians 5:17). Our prayers to the Lord should be natural and spontaneous, spoken in an attitude of praise and thanksgiving. When necessary, intercession should be made with urgency. James tells us that *"the prayer of a righteous man is powerful and effective."* He is encouraging his readers to pray as well as to practice righteousness.

The Wandering Brother

James concludes his letter with an appeal to his readers to take responsibility for those who have fallen by the wayside. Physically ill people usually know they need assistance; but people who are self-deceived and spiritually ill may be unaware of the peril they face. Although our help may not always be appreciated, James insists we have a responsibility to go after someone who strays away from the truth. Our efforts may lead to the salvation of that person's soul and the application of Christ's sacrificial blood to cover all his or her sins.

Personalize this lesson.

☑ The book of James teaches us the necessity of practicing our faith in Jesus Christ and points out many ways to demonstrate that faith. We have learned that *"faith without deeds is dead"* (2:26), but we must also realize that deeds without faith are useless. Faith—not works—forms the basis of our lives in Christ (Ephesians 2:8-9). Our hope of glory lies in what Christ did—not in what we do. That hope is born in us when we are born again (John 3:3-8). As we believe in Jesus, He comes to dwell within us. By faith we begin to live the Christian life (Galatians 3:1-3), which is impossible to do unless we allow Christ to live it through us! We must daily relinquish control of our lives—our tongues and our money, our todays and tomorrows—to God and ask Him to give us wisdom, power, patience, and self-control. Will you ask Him to help you let Jesus live more of His life through you as a result of studying this book? Think back to lesson 1 and the areas you wanted to grow in. Are you already starting to see some changes? Thank God for what He is doing and trust Him to continue to do that good work in you.

Small Group Leader's Guide

While *Engaging God's Word* is great for personal study, it is generally even more effective and enjoyable when studied with others. Studying with others provides different perspectives and insights, care, prayer support, and fellowship that studying on your own does not. Depending on your personal circumstances, consider studying with your family or spouse, with a friend, in a Sunday school, with a small group at church, work, or in your neighborhood, or in a mentoring relationship.

In a traditional Community Bible Study class, your study would involve a proven four-step method: personal study, a small group discussion facilitated by a trained leader, a lecture covering the passage of Scripture, and a written commentary about the same passage. *Engaging God's Word* provides two of these four steps with the study questions and commentary. When you study with a group, you add another of these—the group discussion. And if you enjoy teaching, you could even provide a modified form of the fourth, the lecture, which in a small group setting might be better termed a wrap-up talk.

Here are some suggestions to help leaders facilitate a successful group study.

1. Decide how long you would like each group meeting to last. For a very basic study, without teaching, time for fellowship, or group prayer, plan on one hour. If you want to allow for fellowship before the meeting starts, add at least 15 minutes. If you plan to give a short teaching, add 15 or 20 minutes. If you also want time for group prayer, add another 10 or 15 minutes. Depending on the components you include for your group, each session will generally last between one and two hours.

2. Set a regular time and place to meet. Meeting in a church classroom or a conference room at work is fine. Meeting in a home is also a good option, and sometimes more relaxed and comfortable.

3. Publicize the study and/or personally invite people to join you.

4. Begin praying for those who have committed to come. Continue to pray for them individually throughout the course of the study.

5. Make sure everyone has his or her own book at least a week before you meet for the first time.

6. Encourage group members to read the first lesson and do the questions before they come to the group meeting.

7. Prepare your own lesson.

8. Prepare your wrap-up talk, if you plan to give one. Here is a simple process for developing a wrap-up talk:

   a. Divide the passage you are studying into two or three divisions. Jot down the verses for each division and describe the content of each with one complete sentence that answers the question, "What is the passage about?"

   b. Decide on the central idea of your wrap-up talk. The central idea is the life-changing principle found in the passage that you believe God wants to implant in the hearts and minds of your group. The central idea answers the question, "What does God want us to learn from this passage?"

   c. Provide one illustration that would make your central idea clear and meaningful to your group. This could be an illustration from your own life, or a story you've read or heard somewhere else.

   d. Suggest one application that would help your group put the central idea into practice.

   e. Choose an aim for your wrap-up talk. The aim answers the question, "What does God want us to do about it?" It encourages specific change in your group's lives, if they choose to respond to the central idea of the passage. Often it takes the form of a question you will ask your group: "Will you, will I choose to … ?"

9. Show up early to the study so you can arrange the room, set up the refreshments (if you are serving any), and welcome people as they arrive.

10. Whether your meeting includes a fellowship time or not, begin the discussion time promptly each week. People appreciate it when you respect their time. Transition into the discussion with prayer, inviting God to guide the discussion time and minister personally to each person present.

11. Model enthusiasm to the group. Let them know how excited you are about what you are learning—and your eagerness to hear what God is teaching them.

12. As you lead through the questions, encourage everyone to participate, but don't force anyone. If one or two people tend to dominate the discussion, encourage quieter ones to participate by saying something like, "Let's hear from someone who hasn't shared yet." Resist the urge to teach during discussion time. This time is for your group to share what they have been discovering.

13. Try to allow time after the questions have been discussed to talk about the "Apply what you have learned," "Think about" and "Personalize this lesson" sections. Encourage your group members in their efforts to partner with God in allowing Him to transform their lives.

14. Transition into the wrap-up talk, if you are doing one (see number 8).

15. Close in prayer. If you have structured your group to allow time for prayer, invite group members to pray for themselves and one another, especially focusing on the areas of growth they would like to see in their lives as a result of their study. If you have not allowed time for group prayer, you as leader can close this time.

16. Before your group finishes their final lesson, start praying and planning for what your next *Engaging God's Word* study will be.

About Community Bible Study

For almost 40 years Community Bible Study has taught the Word of God through in-depth, community-based Bible studies. With nearly 700 classes in the United States as well as classes in more than 70 countries, Community Bible Study purposes to be an "every-person's Bible study, available to all."

Classes for men, women, youth, children, and even babies, are all designed to make members feel loved, cared for, and accepted— regardless of age, ethnicity, socio-economic status, education, or church membership. Because Bible study is most effective in one's heart language, Community Bible Study curriculum has been translated into more than 50 languages.

Community Bible Study makes every effort to stand in the center of the mainstream of historic Christianity, concentrating on the essentials of the Christian faith rather than denominational distinctives. Community Bible Study respects different theological views, preferring to focus on helping people to know God through His Word, grow deeper in their relationships with Jesus, and be transformed into His likeness.

Community Bible Study's focus ... is to glorify God by providing in-depth Bible studies and curriculum in a Christ-centered, grace-filled, and philosophically safe environment.

Community Bible Study's passion ... is the transformation of individuals, families, communities, and generations through the power of God's Word, making disciples of the Lord Jesus Christ.

Community Bible Study's relationship with local churches ... is one of support and respect. Community Bible Study classes are composed of people from many different churches; they are designed to complement and not compete with the ministry of the local church. Recognizing that the Lord has chosen the local church as His primary channel of ministry, Community Bible Study encourages class members to belong to and actively support their local churches and to be servants and leaders in their congregations.

Do you want to experience lasting transformation in your life? Are you ready to go deeper in God's Word? There is probably a Community Bible Study near you! Find out by visiting www.findmyclass.org or scan the QR code on this page.

For more information:

Call   800-826-4181

Email info@communitybiblestudy.org

Web   www.communitybiblestudy.org

Class www.findmyclass.org

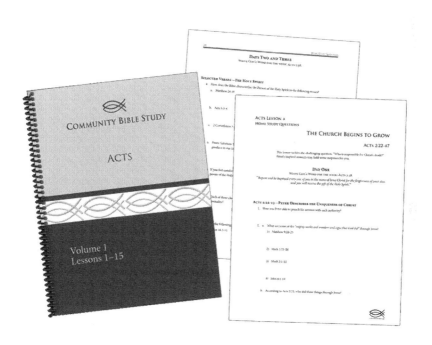

Where will your next Bible study adventure take you?

Engage Bible Studies help you discover the joy
and the richness of God's Word and apply it your life. Check out
these titles for your next adventure:

Engaging God's Word: Genesis

Engaging God's Word: Daniel

Engaging God's Word: Mark

Engaging God's Word: Luke

Engaging God's Word: Galatians

Engaging God's Word: Ephesians

Engaging God's Word: Philippians

Engaging God's Word: Colossians

Engaging God's Word: Hebrews

Engaging God's Word: 1 & 2 Peter

Engaging God's Word: James

Engaging God's Word: Revelation

New adventures available soon:

Engaging God's Word: Acts

Engaging God's Word: Ruth & Esther

Engaging God's Word: Job

Engaging God's Word: 1 & 2 Thessalonians

Also coming soon:

Engage Bible Studies in Spanish!
Available at Amazon.com and in fine bookstores.
Visit engagebiblestudies.com

Made in the USA
Charleston, SC
11 May 2013

Lesson 4

A Living Hope
1 Thessalonians 4:13–5:11

❖ 1 Thessalonians 4:13-15—Concerns for Those Who Sleep

1. What seems to be the concern of the church according to 1 Thessalonians 4:13-15?

   what happens when people die

2. What is the hope that allows Christians to grieve differently than those without hope?

   Jesus died + rose again and will come to get us and raise those who are asleep.

❖ 1 Thessalonians 4:16-18—Description of the Lord's Coming

3. What are the truths recorded in 1 Thessalonians 4:16-17?

   The Lord himself will come down from heaven with a loud shout, voice of the archangel, and trumpet and dead in christ will rise first

4. In 4:18, what command is given after *"therefore"*?

   encourage one another

   we will be caught up together with them in the clouds to meet the Lord in the air.

5. How would these things encourage you if you had just lost a loved one?

HOPE, PROMISE of Christ's return

❖ 1 Thessalonians 5:1-4—Concerns About the Day of the Lord

6. Paul begins verse 1 with the introduction, "*Now concerning the times and seasons, brothers.*" What question do you think he is responding to in this section?

"When will this happen"?

7. Why does Paul say to the Thessalonians "*you have no need to have anything written to you*" about the day of the Lord?

They should already know this

8. What will the day of the Lord be like for those in darkness?

↓ pain and destruction
↓ sudden

9. What does 2 Peter 3:10-18 add to your understanding of the day of the Lord?

Not the same as rapture ???

❖ 1 Thessalonians 5:5-8—Living as Children of the Light

10. What differences in lifestyle does Paul note between children of light and those of the darkness?

_____

_____

_____

_____

11. What does Paul tell children of day to put on in verse 8 and how is this helpful to them?

_____

_____

_____

12. Why do you think Paul pairs faith and love with a breastplate and hope of salvation with a helmet?

_____

_____

_____

13. Of the two things that Paul wants you to put on, which do you need the most today and why?

_____

_____

_____

❖ 1 Thessalonians 5:9-11—Assurance of the Future

14. How does Paul reassure the Thessalonians concerning their future?

_____

_____

_____

15. Do you have this assurance? Explain.

_____

_____

_____

_____

16. What are some ways you can encourage someone who is concerned about life after death or the return of the Lord?

_____

_____

_____

_____

_____

_____

Apply what you have learned. We are not to be ignorant or fearful concerning the return of the Lord. But neither can His return occupy us in endless speculation or argument or worry. It will occur. It will take the world by surprise. The true church will be caught up to be with the Lord forever. Until then, how do we live? Awake. Alert. Self-controlled. Encouraging and building up others. When we live this way, we can be confident that when He comes we will be ready. Is there anything you can do to live more consistently in these ways?

A Living Hope
1 Thessalonians 2:17–4:12

This short letter gives information concerning the second coming of Christ. Jesus specifically said that no one knows the day or hour but God alone. Many avoid this subject because throughout church history multitudes of "date setters" proclaimed that Christ would return at a certain time, and they were embarrassingly wrong. Although Paul and the Thessalonians did not name a day for Christ's return, they longed for it and expected that He might come back while they were still alive.

For the Thessalonian believers, the questions Paul addressed came quite naturally. If Christ did return while they were still alive, what would happen to those who had already died? How would Christ's return affect them? Had they missed out on the blessing? Would they rise from the dead later?

Hope in the Midst of Sorrow (1 Thessalonians 4:13-14)

"We do not want you to be uninformed ... about those who are asleep, that you may not grieve as others do who have no hope" (4:13). Death, for believers, is sometimes called sleep. For the pagan world, it was considered neither a restful nor temporary *sleep*. For them, death was the cessation of life; nothing existed beyond it. Documents and grave markers of the ancient pagan world reveal the bleak despair that accompanied death. The Roman poet Catullus wrote: "The sun can set and rise again, but once our brief light sets there is one unending night to be slept through." By contrast, Paul told the Philippians he longed to depart this life to *"be with Christ."* Likewise, Jesus told the thief who died beside Him, *"Today you will be with Me in Paradise"* (Luke 23:43). It is certain that believers go directly into God's presence when they die.

The Basis of Hope (1 Thessalonians 4:15-18)

What is the basis of the Thessalonians' hope? The assurance of hope for both the living and dead in Christ rests on the word of Jesus Himself: *"I am the resurrection and the life. Whoever believes in Me, though he die, yet shall he live, and everyone who lives and believes in Me shall never die"* (John 11:25-26). Paul gives a wonderful description of the resurrection in verses 16-17: *"The Lord himself will descend from heaven with a cry of command, with the voice of an archangel, and with the sound of the trumpet of God. And the dead in Christ will rise first. Then we who are alive, who are left, will be caught up together with them in the clouds to meet the Lord in the air, and so we will always be with the Lord."*

Christian teaching clearly describes the resurrection of the body (1 Corinthians 15:51-54). Greek philosophers taught there would be no physical existence in future life—only a nonmaterial soul. However, new bodies will replace our decaying bodies and through eternity, believers will have perfected bodies and purified souls. As Paul wrote, *"We await a Savior, the Lord Jesus Christ, who will transform our lowly body to be like His glorious body"* (Philippians 3:20-21).

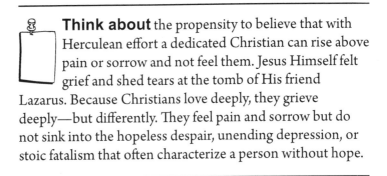

Think about the propensity to believe that with Herculean effort a dedicated Christian can rise above pain or sorrow and not feel them. Jesus Himself felt grief and shed tears at the tomb of His friend Lazarus. Because Christians love deeply, they grieve deeply—but differently. They feel pain and sorrow but do not sink into the hopeless despair, unending depression, or stoic fatalism that often characterize a person without hope.

Paul describes Christ's return as a phenomenal event. Jesus' arrival at His first coming was unquestionably wondrous yet relatively unobtrusive. In contrast, the second coming will be startling, sudden, and amazing. Paul concludes, fittingly, *"Therefore encourage one other with these words"* (1 Thessalonians 4:18). What a difference the truth of Christ's return and Christian hope make!

The Day of the Lord (1 Thessalonians 5:1-11)

Paul shifts to a different aspect of Christ's second coming: *"the times and the seasons"* (5:1). The Greek word for *times* (*chronos*) refers to *lengths of time*. How long will various eras of history last? The Greek word for *"seasons"* (*kairos*) refers to *a definite moment*, a strategic point in time. When is the exact date of Christ's return? *"You yourselves are fully aware that the day of the Lord will come like a thief in the night"* (5:2). Paul does not set a date; the day of the Lord will come suddenly and without warning.

The *"day of the Lord"* is an Old Testament phrase describing a future cosmic judgment of Israel and the world. Its purpose was to judge the sins of the world, and to free God's people from the power and effect of sin. This theme of sudden judgment fits Paul's description. *"While people are saying, 'There is peace and security,' then sudden destruction will come upon them as labor pains come upon a pregnant woman, and they will not escape"* (5:3). The event is as unpredictable as the onset of a woman's labor. However, Paul offers encouragement: *"But you are not in darkness … for that day to surprise you like a thief. For you are all children of light, children of the day"* (5:4-5).

In contrast to those who are *"of the night"* (5:7), Paul says that believers *"belong to the day"* (5:8). They are to behave like those who live in daylight, being *"awake"* and *"sober"* (5:6, 8). *"Awake"* means alert, watchful, ready to respond to God and what He is doing. *"Sober"* is the Greek word *nepho*, meaning *sobriety, self control*. Christians must be fully alert and not let the cry of *"peace and security"* dull their spiritual sensitivity.

Paul describes believers as soldiers, armed with breastplates of *"faith and love"* and a helmet—*"the hope of salvation"* (5:8). Believers are not destined for God's wrathful judgment, which the day of the Lord will bring on those who have rejected Christ. Instead, Jesus *"died for us so that … we might live with Him"* (5:10). All believers will be with the Lord in heaven and the new earth for eternity (Revelation 21:1). Paul concludes, *"Therefore encourage one another and build one another up"* (5:11). As we encourage each other, we can stand in the battle of life.

Personalize this lesson.

✓ As the Thessalonians learned to walk in their new faith, they were perplexed with questions about death and life after death. Perhaps they were experiencing the death of one of their own and wondered what difference their faith in Jesus made during times of sorrow. What did it mean to *"not grieve as others do who have no hope"*? Perhaps that has been a question you have grappled with too, as you have grieved the death of someone you love. As you consider this week's lesson, what concrete hope will you tuck away in your soul to give you comfort in the face of death?

Encouragement and Warning
1 Thessalonians 5:12–2 Thessalonians 1:12

Memorize God's Word: 1 Thessalonians 5:16-18.

❖ 1 Thessalonians 5:12-22—Instructions

1. Why are leaders to be respected?

2. How can you apply this exhortation *"to respect those who labor among you"*?

3. What commands does Paul give in this passage?

4. Which commands do you find most challenging?

5. How could you incorporate them into your life?

_____

_____

_____

❖ 1 Thessalonians 5:23-28—Prayers and Benediction

6. According to verses 23-24, what does God do for those who believe?

_____

_____

7. How does this encourage you to live out the previous verses (5:12-24)?

_____

_____

_____

8. What is the significance of Paul identifying all three parts of the human being?

_____

_____

_____

9. How are these three parts involved in the sanctifying process?

_____

_____

_____

❖ 2 Thessalonians 1:1-10—God's Righteous Judgment

10. Why is Paul grateful for the Thessalonians (verses 3-4)?

_____

_____

11. What does Paul say will happen *"when the Lord Jesus is revealed from heaven"?*

_____

_____

_____

12. Paul says God's judgment is righteous (verse 5). How would you explain this to someone who struggles with a God who inflicts vengeance on others (verse 8)?

_____

_____

_____

_____

13. How would knowing these things help the persecuted Thessalonians not repay vengeance? (See also Romans 12:12-20.)

_____

_____

_____

_____

❖ 2 Thessalonians 1:11-12—Paul's Prayer

14. Throughout these letters Paul is praying for the Thessalonians. What is his prayer from these verses?

_____

_____

_____

15. How does his prayer demonstrate his understanding that both God and the individual have important roles in a believer's faithfulness?

_____

_____

_____

16. According to verse 12, when God answers Paul's prayer what will be the result?

_____

_____

_____

17. How might the name of Jesus *"be glorified in you"*?

_____

_____

_____

_____

_____

_____

Apply what you have learned. Paul reveals his delight in the Thessalonians when he discloses *"we ourselves boast about you in the churches of God for your steadfastness and faith in all your persecutions and in the afflictions that you are enduring"* (2 Thessalonians 1:4). Clearly Paul understands and empathizes with their suffering. He desires to affirm and encourage their commitment to faith. These words demonstrate for us how to *"encourage the fainthearted and help the weak"* (1 Thessalonians 5:14). Think about persons in your life who would benefit from your words of encouragement. How might you let them know that you notice their devotion to God and loyalty to walk with Him—especially in the midst of difficult times?

Encouragement and Warning
1 Thessalonians 5:12–2 Thessalonians 1:12

Corporate Life in the Body of Christ
(1 Thessalonians 5:12-28)

Paul charges the Thessalonians to "*respect those who labor among you and are over you in the Lord and admonish you*" (5:12). Possibly some Christians had quit working while they waited for Christ's return and resisted the authority of the church leaders. Paul urges the entire church to "*admonish the idle*" (5:14) while also encouraging the fainthearted and helping the weak. The Greek noun translated *fainthearted* described *a timid or inadequate person*, perhaps those who were tempted to give up because of social pressure and persecution. "*The weak*" were probably emotionally and spiritually weak. Paul says to encourage and help the timid and weak, but to sternly warn the idle being "*patient with them all.*"

Going further, Paul says to "*see that no one repays anyone evil for evil, but always seek to do good to one another and to everyone*" (5:15). We are to resist retaliation when someone hurts us. Paul also commands attitudes of joy, prayer, and thankfulness. The command to "*pray without ceasing*" (5:17) uses a Greek word that describes *a hacking cough or anything recurring constantly*. We cannot pray every moment of our lives, but we are to pray frequently.

Continuing, Paul instructs the believer not to "*quench the Spirit. Do not despise prophecies, but test everything; hold fast what is good*" (5:19-21). Apparently some believers were stirring up the congregation with speculations about the second coming, causing members to reject all prophetic utterances. Paul urges the Thessalonians not to reject prophecies, but to test them, because prophecies can be fabricated. "*Abstain from every form of evil*" (5:22) applies most directly to rejecting false teaching. However, evil comes in a variety of forms, and this warning applies to life in general.

Paul concludes praying that God will sanctify them totally, making them perfectly holy in their spirit, soul, and body. God desires to sanctify the entire person. A state of perfect holiness will be reached only at Christ's return, when even the believer's physical body will be changed. This is also a call to holiness, an exhortation to resemble in life what will be completed only at the Second Coming.

Think about how most people's hopes are tied to life's uncertainties; they hope for improved health, mended marriages, children they can be proud of, more money. If what they hope for, dream of, and pray about does not materialize, they are devastated. Biblical hope, on the other hand, focuses on what we can be certain of—God's faithfulness to sanctify us, His presence with us in our current circumstances, our salvation in heaven, and God's ultimate victory over evil. Such certain hope keeps us positive even in the worst situations. The Thessalonians had joy because they hoped in Jesus Christ and expectantly awaited His return. When our faith and hope are properly placed in God, we, too, can have joy.

Reward and Judgment at the Second Coming (2 Thessalonians 1:1-10)

The writing of 2 Thessalonians follows the first letter by only a few months. The messengers who delivered 1 Thessalonians returned with news of the church and misgivings about speculative, unbalanced teachings that some people advocated concerning the day of the Lord and Christ's return. Paul addresses this and continues to encourage them in the face of persecution. The Thessalonians' faith, love, and endurance are *"evidence of the righteous judgment of God, that you may be considered worthy of the kingdom of God"* (1:5). Their strength and faith show the world that God is victorious over evil here and now, foreshadowing His final conquest at the Second Coming.

Being gloriously ushered into Christ's kingdom contrasts sharply with what will befall those who reject God (1:6-10). In the Old Testament, *the day of the Lord* emphasized two themes: the blessing of God's people and the punishment of the wicked. For most of us the Scriptures about blessings are no problem, but many people struggle with the severe statements in both Testaments that speak of judgment and everlasting punishment.

Throughout the Scriptures, the tension of truth exists: God's justice both commends and condemns. Just as salvation is grounded in God's mercy and love, so God's condemnation is grounded in His justice and holiness. God does not capriciously or impulsively bring punishment and judgment on people. He is a righteous God, and in Him there is no error. We face a choice: Either respond to the promise of eternal life through the Lord Jesus or reject the good news of salvation with the consequences of "*eternal destruction*" and the absence of God—who alone can deliver us from evil. In His love, God sent His own Son to suffer the penalty of sin in our place. Through faith in Him, we escape eternal destruction (1 Thessalonians 5:3-11). We must see that God takes no pleasure in the death of the wicked (Ezekiel 18:23). Jesus speaks of joy in heaven over one sinner who repents, but He felt deepest grief over those who rejected Him (Matthew 23:37).

Paul's Prayer (2 Thessalonians 1:11-12)

Paul again prays for his deeply loved converts, that "*our God may make you worthy of His calling*" (1:11). A worthy life is not one deemed good enough to earn salvation, but one lived as a result of receiving salvation. So here, Paul reminds the young believers that the gift of grace creates an expectation of worthy response. He also prays "*that our God … may fulfill every resolve for good and every work of faith by His power*" (2 Thessalonians 1:11). Paul's desire is that the Thessalonians will act by God's power to accomplish the good purposes they have begun and that God will bring to completion every act prompted by faith—"*so that the name of our Lord Jesus may be glorified in you, and you in Him*" (1:12).

Personalize this lesson.

✓ Paul gives practical advice at the end of 1 Thessalonians. Verses 16-18 call us to *"rejoice always, pray without ceasing, and give thanks in all circumstances."* Any one of these commands by itself is difficult to live—we're simply not naturally inclined that way. But Paul packages them together and concludes that *"this is the will of God"* for us. To be always joyful and thankful, and to pray without stopping, requires a conscious decision on our part. Consider the following questions as you talk with God about His will for you. How can you build into your daily life the discipline of thankfulness? How are thankfulness and joy connected? How might maintaining a prayerful relationship with God increase your sense of joy and gratitude?

Lesson 6

Stand Firm in Truth
2 Thessalonians 2–3

❖ 1 Thessalonians 2:1-8—Man of Lawlessness

1. What has caused the Thessalonians to become alarmed?

2. What is the nature of their concerns and confusion?

3. What perspective does Paul offer (2:3)?

4. What does this impostor wish to achieve?

5. What will finally happen to the *"man of lawlessness"*?

❖ 2 Thessalonians 2:9-17—Loving the Truth

6. Who energizes the *"man of lawlessness"*?

_____

_____

_____

7. According to verses 10-12, why is loving the truth so important?

_____

_____

_____

8. Do you think there is a difference between believing the truth and loving the truth? If so, explain.

_____

_____

_____

9. In view of the people Paul just described in verses 10-12, why do you think Paul felt such gratitude concerning the Thessalonians?

_____

_____

_____

10. How does Paul both encourage and exhort them in verses 13-15?

_____

_____

_____

11. What aspect of Paul's blessing in verses 16-17 would you like to pray for yourself? And pray for someone else?

_____

_____

_____

❖ 2 Thessalonians 3:1-5—Prayer for Them and for Us

12. Paul asked the Thessalonians to pray for him. For what does he request prayer?

_____

_____

_____

13. What is Paul's way of dealing with evil people and the evil one?

_____

_____

_____

14. If Timothy came to visit you and reported back to Paul, what evidence in your life would he see that would give him *"confidence in the Lord about you"*?

_____

_____

_____

_____

❖ 2 Thessalonians 3:6-15—Living in Community

15. This is the second time Paul has warned about idleness (1 Thessalonians 5:14) among the believers. From this passage and your own thoughts, why do you think Paul emphasized this?

_____

_____

_____

16. How does Paul say to treat those who are disobedient (3:14-15)?

_____

_____

_____

17. What is Paul trying to accomplish with this instruction?

_____

_____

18. How might we apply this instruction?

_____

_____

2 Thessalonians 3:16-18—A Blessing of Peace

19. Why do you think Paul chose the particular blessing he used in 3:16 to close his letter?

_____

_____

_____

20. Can you think of a specific situation in which you would like the Lord to bless you in a similar way?

_____

_____

_____

Apply what you have learned. The Thessalonians were caught up in their questions about the lawless one and the second coming of Christ. Paul addresses their concerns and then turns their attention back to their daily walk of faith. *"May our Lord Jesus Christ Himself ... encourage your hearts and strengthen you in every good deed and word"* (2:16-17). What an encouraging perspective to think that Jesus will strengthen us in every action we do and every word we say! This seems to be the answer to Paul's admonition to, *"not grow weary in doing good"* (3:13). As you consider what you will say or what you will do, how can you access Jesus' strength?

Lesson 6 Commentary

Stand Firm in Truth
2 Thessalonians 2–3

The Man of Lawlessness (2 Thessalonians 2:1-4)

A false teaching troubled the Thessalonians and may have caused the idleness Paul previously warned against. Paul writes, *"Concerning the coming of our Lord Jesus Christ and our being gathered together to Him, we ask you, brothers, not to be quickly shaken in mind or alarmed, either by a spirit or a spoken word, or a letter seeming to be from us, to the effect that the day of the Lord has come"* (2:1-2). The source of this teaching that the day of the Lord had already arrived may have been a false prophecy, a fake report, or a forged letter written by Paul's Jewish enemies.

Such a view had disturbing implications—that the end of the age was virtually upon them and all long-term plans were needless. It justified quitting work and being idle. This false report suggested that the Thessalonians, along with the rest of the world, were entering the worst period of suffering in all history. Paul responds to this confusion by reminding the readers of his initial instruction: Before the Lord's return, the rebellion will occur and the man of lawlessness will be revealed. Satan will make his final effort to overthrow the purposes of God. Paul's point is that this man has not yet come, and therefore the second coming of Jesus Christ has not taken place. The time has been fixed by God and certain events must first take place. This man of lawlessness will attempt two things: (1) He will exalt himself and oppose everything that is worshiped, setting himself up as God in the temple. (2) He will try to utterly confuse the understanding of truth, successfully deceiving *"those who are perishing"* (2:10).

From Paul's time until now, many have theorized about who this man of lawlessness might be, with ideas ranging from religious leaders to world dictators. But just who this person is, or when exactly he will be recognized, is not at all clear from Scripture. Christians need to be careful about anyone who takes for himself God's authority and worship and impresses others by the use of supernatural power.

Think about the importance of loving truth. Paul didn't say that those who would fall for the *"wicked deception"* of the *"man of lawlessness"* would be uncommonly foolish or godless. Their fatal mistake lay simply in not loving truth. People who love the truth are not easily deceived. They test ideas and question the validity of the information that comes their way, using Scripture as their plumb line. And what they do believe, they believe with unshakable confidence. Take a moment to ponder where truth already influences your life. Is it present in the words you speak? In the messages and media you expose yourself to? In the advice you follow? As you pursue a greater love for what is true, you'll grow closer to God—the original Source of truth. In the wisdom He gives you, you will not fall victim to the falsehoods you encounter.

His Delay and His Doom (2 Thessalonians 2:5-12)

Paul explains that *"the lawless one"* will be *"restrained"* by *"He who now restrains it … until He is out of the way"* (2:7). Who or what restrains this evil one until the proper time? Scholars have suggested every conceivable answer: the Roman government, the Jewish state, law and order, Satan, even Paul. Two major positions emerge. First is the restraining work of the Holy Spirit, for God alone has adequate power to restrain the antichrist; so the Holy Spirit must remove His restraining power from the world and allow human sinfulness to run its full course. The second view is that the existence of government established by God is itself the restraining agency.

As powerful as the *"man of lawlessness"* is, at the second coming of Christ he will be utterly destroyed. In the meantime, the *"mystery of lawlessness is already at work"* (2 Thessalonians 2:7). At the time Paul wrote this letter, the forces of both iniquity and restraint were in combat for influence in the world—a spiritual warfare that continues today (Ephesians 6:12).

Paul gives a final description of the *"man of lawlessness"*: His coming will be accompanied by all kinds of counterfeit miracles, signs, and wonders, and by every sort of evil. People will embrace this imitation Christ, refusing to love the truth and be saved. *"Therefore God sends them a strong delusion, so that they may believe what is false, in order that all may be condemned who did not believe the truth"* (2:11-12). God simply releases them to the full consequences of their choice. The result is not only that the *"man of lawlessness"* is able to come to power, but that when given a choice between him or Jesus Christ, *"those who are perishing"* (2:10) will choose to worship and follow the *"man of lawlessness"* because of their sinfulness and blindness.

Paul's Final Words and Warnings (2 Thessalonians 2:12–3:18)

In case some Thessalonians fear being deceived, Paul assures them, *"God chose you as the firstfruits to be saved, through sanctification by the Spirit and belief in the truth"* (2:13). He encourages them not to waver but stand firm, asking God to encourage and strengthen them. They are to *"hold to the traditions that you were taught by us, either by our spoken word or by our letter"* (2:15).

Paul values the young Thessalonian Christians' prayers and asks them to pray for his protection and that of his fellow missionaries. He has told them hard truths about the possibility of deception; now he promises that God will protect them from the evil one and help them to persevere. Sadly, some believers get so enamored with the study of Satan and the antichrist that they grow fearful. God wants believers to focus on Jesus Christ, not the powers of darkness.

Paul now goes into more detail about the *idle*. His first letter says to warn them, but here they are to be separated from fellowship. They should not be enabled in their idleness or regarded as enemies, but warned as brothers. The aim is to encourage them *"to earn their own living"* (3:12).

Appropriately, Paul prays God's peace over the Thessalonians. He usually dictated his letters to fellow believers who acted as secretaries, but he writes with his own hand at the end of this letter, to assure the readers of his authorship. Perhaps a forged letter had come with false teachings about the second coming. Paul clearly takes ownership of the end time teaching laid out in 1 and 2 Thessalonians.

Personalize this lesson.

✓ Through the centuries, believers in various lands have suffered such prolonged periods of deprivation or persecution that they believed the day of the Lord was upon them. But any teaching about the timing of the day of the Lord and the identity of the *"man of lawlessness"* must be carefully examined. To avoid being deceived, we must *"hold firm to the trustworthy word as taught"* (Titus 1:9).

Because Jesus' teachings are constantly being distorted and mixed with falsehoods, we must base our understanding of the last days on what we find in Scripture. Our trustworthy God has made sure that the knowledge contained in the Bible is sufficient for the challenges we face. John says that what he included in his Gospel is sufficient for us to find salvation in Christ: *"Jesus did many other signs in the presence of the disciples, which are not written in this book; but these are written so that you may believe that Jesus is the Christ, the Son of God, and that by believing you may have life in His name"* (John 20:30-31). We are also assured that *"[God's] divine power has given us everything we need for life and godliness through our knowledge of Him"* (2 Peter 1:3, NIV). Even though the Bible offers vast amounts of spiritual understanding and wisdom, many of our "what?" and "how?" questions will have to go unanswered until we see our Lord Jesus *"face to face"* (1 Corinthians 13:12).

How do you handle questions left unanswered in Scripture? Our response to unanswered questions may be a reflection of our trust in God. Paul states that the Lord is faithful. How do we develop hearts that trust God enough to accept that what He has given us in His Word is enough? In what ways are you trusting Him with your unanswered questions?

Small Group Leader's Guide

While *Engaging God's Word* is great for personal study, it is generally even more effective and enjoyable when studied with others. Studying with others provides different perspectives and insights, care, prayer support, and fellowship that studying on your own does not. Depending on your personal circumstances, consider studying with your family or spouse, with a friend, in a Sunday school, with a small group at church, work, or in your neighborhood, or in a mentoring relationship.

In a traditional Community Bible Study class, your study would involve a proven four-step method: personal study, a small group discussion facilitated by a trained leader, a lecture covering the passage of Scripture, and a written commentary about the same passage. *Engaging God's Word* provides two of these four steps with the study questions and commentary. When you study with a group, you add another of these—the group discussion. And if you enjoy teaching, you could even provide a modified form of the fourth, the lecture, which in a small group setting might be better termed a wrap-up talk.

Here are some suggestions to help leaders facilitate a successful group study.

1. Decide how long you would like each group meeting to last. For a very basic study, without teaching, time for fellowship, or group prayer, plan on one hour. If you want to allow for fellowship before the meeting starts, add at least 15 minutes. If you plan to give a short teaching, add 15 or 20 minutes. If you also want time for group prayer, add another 10 or 15 minutes. Depending on the components you include for your group, each session will generally last between one and two hours.

2. Set a regular time and place to meet. Meeting in a church classroom or a conference room at work is fine. Meeting in a home is also a good option, and sometimes more relaxed and comfortable.

3. Publicize the study and/or personally invite people to join you.

4. Begin praying for those who have committed to come. Continue to pray for them individually throughout the course of the study.

5. Make sure everyone has his or her own book at least a week before you meet for the first time.

6. Encourage group members to read the first lesson and do the questions before they come to the group meeting.

7. Prepare your own lesson.

8. Prepare your wrap-up talk, if you plan to give one. Here is a simple process for developing a wrap-up talk:

    a. Divide the passage you are studying into two or three divisions. Jot down the verses for each division and describe the content of each with one complete sentence that answers the question, "What is the passage about?"

    b. Decide on the central idea of your wrap-up talk. The central idea is the life-changing principle found in the passage that you believe God wants to implant in the hearts and minds of your group. The central idea answers the question, "What does God want us to learn from this passage?"

    c. Provide one illustration that would make your central idea clear and meaningful to your group. This could be an illustration from your own life, or a story you've read or heard somewhere else.

    d. Suggest one application that would help your group put the central idea into practice.

    e. Choose an aim for your wrap-up talk. The aim answers the question, "What does God want us to do about it?" It encourages specific change in your group's lives, if they choose to respond to the central idea of the passage. Often it takes the form of a question you will ask your group: "Will you, will I choose to ... ?"

9. Show up early to the study so you can arrange the room, set up the refreshments (if you are serving any), and welcome people as they arrive.

10. Whether your meeting includes a fellowship time or not, begin the discussion time promptly each week. People appreciate it when you respect their time. Transition into the discussion with prayer, inviting God to guide the discussion time and minister personally to each person present.

11. Model enthusiasm to the group. Let them know how excited you are about what you are learning—and your eagerness to hear what God is teaching them.

12. As you lead through the questions, encourage everyone to participate, but don't force anyone. If one or two people tend to dominate the discussion, encourage quieter ones to participate by saying something like, "Let's hear from someone who hasn't shared yet." Resist the urge to teach during discussion time. This time is for your group to share what they have been discovering.

13. Try to allow time after the questions have been discussed to talk about the "Apply what you have learned," "Think about" and "Personalize this lesson" sections. Encourage your group members in their efforts to partner with God in allowing Him to transform their lives.

14. Transition into the wrap-up talk, if you are doing one (see number 8).

15. Close in prayer. If you have structured your group to allow time for prayer, invite group members to pray for themselves and one another, especially focusing on the areas of growth they would like to see in their lives as a result of their study. If you have not allowed time for group prayer, you as leader can close this time.

16. Before your group finishes their final lesson, start praying and planning for what your next *Engaging God's Word* study will be.

About Community Bible Study

For almost 40 years Community Bible Study has taught the Word of God through in-depth, community-based Bible studies. With nearly 700 classes in the United States as well as classes in more than 70 countries, Community Bible Study purposes to be an "every-person's Bible study, available to all."

Classes for men, women, youth, children, and even babies, are all designed to make members feel loved, cared for, and accepted— regardless of age, ethnicity, socio-economic status, education, or church membership. Because Bible study is most effective in one's heart language, Community Bible Study curriculum has been translated into more than 50 languages.

Community Bible Study makes every effort to stand in the center of the mainstream of historic Christianity, concentrating on the essentials of the Christian faith rather than denominational distinctives. Community Bible Study respects different theological views, preferring to focus on helping people to know God through His Word, grow deeper in their relationships with Jesus, and be transformed into His likeness.

Community Bible Study's focus ... is to glorify God by providing in-depth Bible studies and curriculum in a Christ-centered, grace-filled, and philosophically safe environment.

Community Bible Study's passion ... is the transformation of individuals, families, communities, and generations through the power of God's Word, making disciples of the Lord Jesus Christ.

Community Bible Study's relationship with local churches ... is one of support and respect. Community Bible Study classes are composed of people from many different churches; they are designed to complement and not compete with the ministry of the local church. Recognizing that the Lord has chosen the local church as His primary channel of ministry, Community Bible Study encourages class members to belong to and actively support their local churches and to be servants and leaders in their congregations.

Do you want to experience lasting transformation in your life? Are you ready to go deeper in God's Word? There is probably a Community Bible Study near you! Find out by visiting www.findmyclass.org or scan the QR code on this page.

For more information:

Call   800-826-4181

Email info@communitybiblestudy.org

Web   www.communitybiblestudy.org

Class www.findmyclass.org

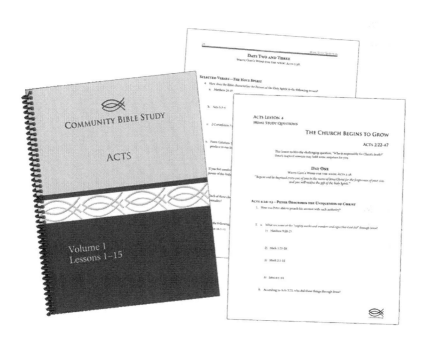

Where will your next Bible study adventure take you?

Engage Bible Studies help you discover the joy and the richness of God's Word and apply it your life.

Check out these titles for your next adventure:

Engaging God's Word: Genesis

Engaging God's Word: Daniel

Engaging God's Word: Job

Engaging God's Word: Mark

Engaging God's Word: Luke

Engaging God's Word: Acts

Engaging God's Word: Romans

Engaging God's Word: Galatians

Engaging God's Word: Ephesians

Engaging God's Word: Philippians

Engaging God's Word: Colossians

Engaging God's Word: 1 & 2 Thessalonians

Engaging God's Word: Hebrews

Engaging God's Word: James

Engaging God's Word: 1 & 2 Peter

Engaging God's Word: Revelation

Also coming soon:

Engage Bible Studies in Spanish!

Available at Amazon.com and in fine bookstores.

Visit engagebiblestudies.com

Made in the USA
Charleston, SC
11 May 2013